MAKING PLASTIC PIPE FURNITURE

MAKING PLASTIC PIPE FURNITURE

MAX AND CHARLOTTE ALTH

Illustrated by Max Alth

EVEREST HOUSE
PUBLISHERS
NEW YORK

Library of Congress Cataloging in Publication Data:

Alth, Max, 1917–
    Making plastic pipe furniture.

    Includes index.
    1. Plastics craft. 2. Plastic furniture.
3. Polyvinyl chloride. I. Alth, Charlotte. II. Title.
TT297.5.A45 1981 684.1′06 81-3158
ISBN: 0-89696-087-0   AACR2

Copyright © 1981 by Max and Charlotte Alth
All Rights Reserved
Published simultaneously in Canada by
Beaverbooks, Don Mills, Ontario
Manufactured in the United States of America
Designed by Judith Lerner
drawings by Michael Prendergast
First Edition
RRD981

DEDICATED TO
Misch
Mike
Darcy
Syme
Kim
Arrabella
Mendle
and all other home craftsmen

Contents

MAKING PLASTIC PIPE FURNITURE

Foreword

IN RECENT YEARS, plastic has become something of a dirty word to environmentalists and clean-earth people. Their objection to this man-made substance is not that it is not found in nature, but that it is not biodegradable and that it does not rust—oxidize. All organic substances can be and are broken down into simpler substances by bacterial action; they rot. Even some nonorganic substances—such as motor oil—are digested by microbes in time. Thus a tin can tossed carelessly into the forest will eventually rust back into the earth and disappear, but a plastic cup or bottle will not. Plastic is tough. It resists sunlight, wind, rain, frost, and microbes.

It is this very orneriness—its resistance to weather and time, its natural strength plus the ease with which it can be cut and joined and its almost universal availability—that makes plastic pipe an ideal material for many types of furniture.

Without a doubt, plastic-pipe furniture is the simplest, cheapest, strongest, and possibly the most beautiful furniture anyone can build, and this includes everyone with two left thumbs.

We use standard PVC (plastic) water pipe sold in almost all plumbing supply shops. The pipe is cut with a saw and joined to other pieces of pipe by slipping the cut ends into pipe fittings made for the purpose. Each joint can be made permanent with some cement or semipermanent with a screw or left as is for quick assembly and disassembly.

The cost of the pipe and fittings is small compared to the cost of an identical piece of plastic-pipe furniture manufactured by furniture companies, or of standard wood and metal furniture. And in addition to the tremendous savings possible, you can easily design and construct plastic-pipe furniture to your own individual tastes and needs. Each piece of plastic-pipe furniture is constructed and assembled more or less like the Tinkertoys of our childhood; there was almost no limit to the number of ways in which those pieces of wood could be assembled. And there is almost no limit to the number of different ways one can construct plastic-pipe furniture.

PART 1

CONSTRUCTION AND DESIGN BASICS

1. Materials

ESSENTIALLY, plastic-pipe furniture consists of a pipe frame onto which a number of smaller-diameter pipes, cushions, and flat surfaces such as boards, may be fastened. In almost all the designs offered commercially and here, the pipe frames consist of any number of straight pieces of pipes joined to each other at an angle. Plastic pipe can be bent. However, bending involves additional effort and is therefore generally avoided. (Bending is discussed in chapter 3.)

Each piece of plastic-pipe furniture consists of a pipe frame. The frame carries or supports the balance of the furniture. For example, in the case of a table, the pipe frame supports the tabletop. There are some exceptions, such as clothes trees, but in the main

FURNITURE FRAMES

Plastic's non-degradeable properties become assets when the plastic is used in pipe form for furniture. This chaise has been left outdoors on the author's front lawn for nearly three years without attention.

15

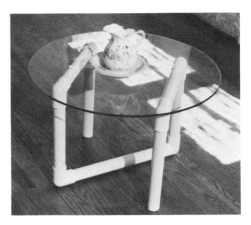

Just a few of the many pipe sizes and fitting types that can be used for making furniture as well as carrying water. Printing can be easily removed with paint remover.

plastic-pipe furniture consists of a frame and either cushions and pads or flat surfaces such as boards and sheets of plastic.

Types of plastic
Some seven different types of plastic pipe are currently employed for plumbing. Each type is compounded according to a different formula, which results in plastics of different qualities. We use PVC—polyvinyl chloride. There is no reason why any of the others cannot be used, except for cost and physical strength. CPVC, which is made of chlorinated polyvinyl chloride and costs more than PVC, can withstand heat somewhat better. It is made to carry hot water at temperatures up to 180 degrees F at full pressure, while PVC is designed to withstand full water pressure at temperatures of no more than 120 degrees. The additional heat strength is not worth the extra cost because furniture is never normally heated to more than 100 degrees. The other plastic-pipe formulations result in pipe that is structurally weaker than PVC, and unless these types are selected for wide-diameter application, they are not sufficiently strong for furniture frames.

Color
Years ago the first Henry Ford said people could order any of his model T's in any color they wished so long as it was funeral black. The same situation almost exists in plastic pipe. There is a choice of three colors, gray, white, and cream, though plumbing supply shops normally do not stock all colors; it is necessary to look for the color one wants. However, plastic pipe in a number of colors can be made—and is—although not for plumbers but for furniture companies. With luck and persistence one may find a furniture manufacturer who may sell some of his colored pipe. If that route proves futile the colored pipe can be made on order from a plastic pipe manufacturer. We don't know how small a

batch they will trouble with, but The Society of the Plastics Industry Inc., 355 Lexington Avenue, New York, N.Y. 10017 can provide the names and addresses of companies making plastic water pipe.

Although PVC and CPVC are classified as rigid, both have a little give or spring at room temperature. At very low temperatures both become brittle. Although they can be left outdoors on the coldest of days, and even used when the temperature is near zero, they lose strength with low temperature and can easily be shattered by a shock—being dropped onto a concrete patio, for example. Repairs to plastic, however, are relatively simple. (This is discussed in chapter 6.)   *Physical characteristics*

Plastic is strongest and toughest at ordinary temperatures. PVC begins to soften slowly as 120 degrees F is passed. CPVC holds its strength to 180 degrees. The softening is not sudden but gradual: the further these formulations are heated beyond their limits the more quickly they will yield under constant pressure. But it is not until they reach a temperature of 350 to 400 degrees that they can easily be bent into any desired shape. However, when these high temperatures are exceeded the plastic will give way suddenly and turn into limp spaghetti. All this means is that plastic pipe furniture requires the same care and consideration given to any furniture: it should not be placed close to an open fire nor near a hot radiator.

Plastic that we use has moderate compression strength and low tensile strength. The pipe can take all the pressure we can place on it, but does not resist bending very well. To keep the pipe frame from bending, horizontal sections are made short, pipe with generous diameter is used, and sometimes the pipe is reinforced internally. (Reinforcement is covered in chapter 4.)

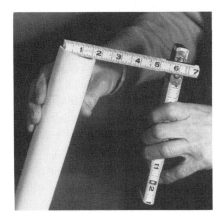

Pipe is sized according to its I.D. (internal diameter) But pipe wall thickness varies from manufacturer so you must check both to be certain you have the correct pipe and fittings.

Pipe Pipe is normally "sized" by its approximate internal diameter.
"size" Thus a one-inch pipe will have an internal diameter of close to
one inch. If the pipe is of metal, its outside diameter will vary
with the metal and application. Thus the O.D. of a 1-inch copper
tube will be 1¼ inches, while the O.D. of a 1-inch iron pipe may
be close to 1½ inches.

Not so with plastic pipe. The O.D. of plastic pipes of varying
wall thicknesses is held steady for all pipes sized the same. Thus
the O.D. of 1-inch DWV (drain, waste, vent) pipe, which has a
thinner wall than standard or pressure plastic pipe, is the same as
the thicker wall-pipe, which also has a 1-inch O.D. The reason is
that all plastic *fittings* are designed to accept plastic pipe. In other
words, all the plastic-pipe fittings are female.

Note that the DWV pipe (some shops call it Schedule 40),
which is lighter than standard PVC pipe, costs less and is entirely
suited to our purpose. Note too that pipes smaller than one inch in
O.D. are not always available in DWV and sometimes can be had
only in CPVC, which is slightly stronger than PVC and costs
more.

Pipe Plastic pipe is normally connected to other plastic pipe by means
fittings of threadless, female fittings. The pipe is the male. All plastic fittings are sized by the size of the pipes they join. Thus a 1-inch
fitting is used with 1-inch pipe. A 1-to-1½-inch fitting connects a
1-inch pipe to a 1½-inch fitting, and so on. Fittings are also described by their shape and purpose. Thus a 3/4-inch 90-degree
elbow connects the ends of two 3/4-inch pipes to form a right
angle. To join the same two pipes at a 45-degree angle, a 45-degree
elbow would be used. A "T" is used to connect three pipe ends to
form a T-shaped joint. When a plastic pipe is to be connected to a
metal pipe or metal fitting, a transition fitting is used. This may be
plastic or metal.

There are literally a hundred different types and sizes of plastic
and transition fittings. However, few plumbing supply shops
carry them all; they stock the fittings most commonly used. This
is why one will see furniture corner-joints made with two T's or a
T and an elbow, and not a single three-pipe fitting that forms a
corner. No shop we could reach carries them. The dealers we
spoke with said they weren't made, although we have seen them
on commercial furniture. In any case, pipe should not be cut in
anticipation of securing specific fittings that may not be available.

All said and done, it's the wise craftsperson who brings along a
piece or pieces of pipe when he goes to purchase fittings. This is
the most reliable way to obtain the desired article: even experienced stock people make mistakes visually sizing fittings.

All plastic pipe comes with data printed on its sides; sometimes in blue, sometimes in red, and occasionally in black. The data include pipe size, generally given as I.D., but occasionally given as O.D., so it's important to read carefully or check size by trying the fittings. And the information will also include pressure and temperature rating, formulation—PVC, CPVC, or whatever—manufacturer's code numbers, and sometimes schedule number and DWV, when applicable.

Cleaning

Some craftspeople choose to let the printing be, considering it to be a high-tech embellishment; a form of art deco. Some, like ourselves, turn the pipe to limit the visibility of the printing to groundhogs and their like, and cleaning only that which will be seen. And some remove all the printing. If the last is done, the pipe should be cleaned before cutting; it's easier that way.

The printing can be removed with nail polish remover, paint remover (oil-base type works best), acetone (available in model airplane shops), or automotive choke cleaner (sold in spray cans at automotive supply stores). We have found the last to work best.

Fluid is applied to the lettering only, remaining in place a minute or so. It is then wiped with a clean rag, in line with the printing, and the rag or the portion of the rag being used is changed as soon as it shows a little color. If the lettering is wiped with a stained rag it will spread the print dye or ink. Work should be done in a well-ventilated room or outdoors: all these solvents give up a terrible stink.

Some of the printing will come clean with one wipe of the solvent-wetted rag. Some will require several applications and rubbings, and some printing ink will hold on for eternity. When two or three applications do not complete the job and if a perfectly clean surface is desired, the printing must be sandpapered off with fine sandpaper. When the unwanted color is gone, the roughened area is rubbed down with steel wool, worked to and fro along the length of the pipe. Fine steel wool will give a surprisingly smooth surface. For an even smoother surface the rubbing should be followed with #500 or #600 sandpaper, applied wet; and for even more shine, with jeweler's rouge, and finally clear auto wax.

Plastic pipe can be painted, but it is not advisable for a number of reasons. The best paint is soft compared to plastic. Thus paint is more easily scratched and abraded. Once scratched through, there is no easy way to cover the exposed plastic. Simply painting over the bare spot will hide it well enough, but it is unlikely that the new paint will match the old exactly; and the new paint will

Painting

always be thicker where it lies on the old. Thus a raised edge will always be seen around the repair spot. For a perfect repair its necessary to paint the spot, let the area dry bone-hard and then sand it down with ultra-fine sandpaper (#600). Then the area is repainted, permitted to dry, and gently sanded perfectly smooth and flat again. Essentially, a paint spotting job on painted plastic must be treated with the same care as spotting a defect in an auto's finish. (If this seems like too much, remember that you and your guests will be much closer to the furniture than you would ordinarily be to your car.)

The surface of the plastic pipe does roughen with time, but since nicks and dents and even gouges do not result in a color change, they are much more difficult to see than the same damages on a painted surface. And surface roughness can be removed by polishing—with ultra-fine sandpaper, followed by jeweler's rouge on a clean cloth, and finished with white jeweler's polish (Tripoli) on another clean cloth.

If one does paint, the surface of the plastic should be prepared by washing it down with unleaded gasoline or turpentine. This is necessary to remove the slight film of wax left on the pipe when the hot plastic was extruded, and the film left by the fingers of anyone who handled the pipe.

Oil-based paints work best, but the others are almost as good and the smoothest results will come if the paint is sprayed on. When spraying one thick coat should not be sought, but rather several thin coats. Care should be taken not to touch the paint's surface between coats.

PANELS   All pipe-frame furniture does not require panels. In some designs the support for cushions and even bodies can be supplied by the use of pipe. However, panels are an integral portion of most pipe-furniture designs. We use panels of wood, glass, and plastic. Leather can also be used, of course, as can canvas, reed, rope, and many other materials. They may be applied over the pipe frame just as they would be applied and fastened to a wood or rattan frame.

Wood   When the panel to be used is more than twelve inches or so wide, plywood is the best material. For one thing, solid panels more than twelve inches wide are increasingly rare and expensive, especially in the more attractive hardwoods. Further, wider, solid boards have a tendency to warp unless they are braced, one way or another. Bracing—for example, with a hidden bolt through the width of the board—is not difficult, but it does add to the complexity and cost of the furniture.

Plywood, on the other hand, will not warp. It is manufactured in many thicknesses and grades, and with a large variety of veneers—top-surface wood. When and where the boards are not exposed to the weather and will be out of sight—say, the panel that supports the mattress on a bed—½-inch construction-grade lumber will serve the purpose. Where the panel will be fastened by screws through its thickness and one side will be visible, 1-inch solid or 3/4-inch plywood, good on one side, should be used. When both sides are visible plywood smooth on both sides is used. Naturally the plywood with both sides covered in attractive hardwood costs more.

As a lower-cost alternative to plywood, chipboard can be used. This is a board made by gluing chips of wood together. In its way it is attractive and can be finished—sanded and varnished—exactly as any other type of wood.

Unless one is an experienced woodworker or has a bench saw, it will be wise to have the lumber yard cut the boards. They may or may not charge for this service; however, with their power saw they can not only do the job much faster but their cuts will be straighter and more accurate. One point of importance: when specifying cutting dimensions, the desired *finished* dimensions must always be stated clearly. It isn't enough to say, for example, that the board ought to be two feet wide. Rather, it must be *exactly* two feet wide. If the yardman asks, "Save the line or on the line?" he should be told to "save the line"—to go as closely as possible without cutting it. A power saw cuts a quarter-inch-wide swath through the lumber. If the blade is centered on the line that edge will be one-eighth inch short. Two cuts on the same board and the board is one-quarter inch shorter than the lines marking its ends or sides.

Glass

For most applications glass makes the ideal panel material. Its surface is hard and smooth and time has no meaning for it. Unfortunately, glass has drawbacks. In thick plate it is very expensive (though seconds with minute imperfections may sometimes be found). Nor can glass be drilled and threaded, at least not by simple means. The glass must be supported and must be held in place by clips or similar devices, or it must be heavy enough to remain in place by weight alone.

Cutting and edge-polishing of thick plate is expensive. If glass panels are used, they should always be worked from the panel to the frame; this should eliminate all need to cut the glass.

Plastic

Sheet plastic can be cut with a saw, drilled, and threaded fairly easily. However, it is more difficult to cut long straight lines through thick-sheet plastic than it is to cut equally long and straight lines through wood. Therefore, the supplier should always cut the sheets.

Plastic panels are expensive; their price is based on weight and as the thickness of the panels increases, so too do the costs.

Plastic is comparatively soft. It is easily scratched and if wiped with a dry, dusty rag too vigorously and too often it will soon be frosted. The acrylics generally used for furniture panels and the like are not fireproof. Drop a match or even a lighted cigarette and the plastic will melt and char. This, of course, will not happen to glass. But plastic does come in colors and there are many panel positions on furniture that never come in contact with matches and cigarettes, and which, also being vertical, do not collect much dust and therefore need little cleaning. So plastic panels do have many attractive, practical applications and are worth considering when one designs furniture.

Marble In the thicknesses that it is normally cut and polished, marble costs considerably less than glass. Marble can be drilled with a masonry bit in an electric drill. This is not as easy as cutting into wood or metal, but it can be done. Drilling means taking one's time and staying away from the edges. Screws can be fastened to marble with Rawl plugs placed in the drilled holes. This means that a marble slab can be placed on a frame with a couple of screws and kept from moving sideways. If this is done, great care should be taken in selecting screw diameter. If the screw is forced and the hole is too close to the edge of the marble, the marble can crack. It will also crack very easily if it has a flaw.

CUSHIONS AND PADS Furniture ads and furniture shops offer a great variety and profusion of cushions, pads, and pillows. This may lead one to believe that almost anything in the desired color, shape, and size is for

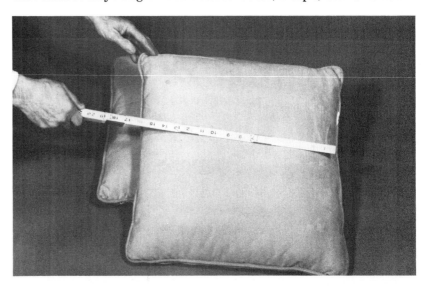

Secure cushions and the like before you begin construction. Check their dimensions when you have them in hand and build accordingly.

sale. Not so. There is a broad choice available in many shops or in a number of shops, but in most instances the cushions, pads, and pillows seen on displayed furniture are *not* sold separately. This means far less choice than one might have imagined, which in turn makes it very important to start with the cushions, pads, and pillows and build around them. Otherwise it may be hard to find the cushioning articles to fit.

Another point. Except for seaboard flotation pillows, we have yet to encounter pillows, pads, and cushions that are truly waterproof. Plastic-pipe furniture will take all the elements, microbes, and bugs that show up in a home or on a patio, but the cushions will not. If left out in the rain they will eventually deteriorate.

2. Tools

MOST CRAFTSPEOPLE already have all the tools they will need. These tools are common enough. If one doesn't have them all there is no point in rushing out to buy them. All the tools mentioned are not required for every project described.

Here is the basic list of tools, more or less in the order of their frequency of use:

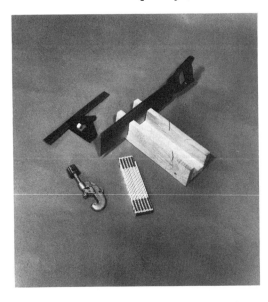

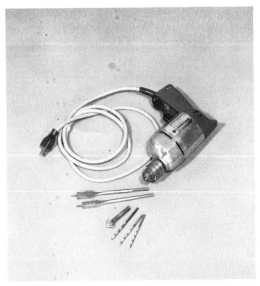

A few of the tools you will find most useful: Miter box and hack saw, combination square, tubing (or pipe) cutter and folding rule.

A ⅜-inch electric drill, two Speedbor wood bits, a counter sink and three twist bits.

Six-foot rule, folding or steel tape
Backsaw or fine-toothed crosscut saw
Miter box—a simple wooden box will do
Electric drill. A 3/8-inch drill is best,
    but one can get by with a ¼-inch drill,
    and use oversize drill bits where needed
Drill bits—sizes depending on the screws
    selected and holes to be drilled
Flat, coarse file
Surform plane
Surform round file
Sandpaper, block of wood
Coping saw (fretsaw)
Hacksaw
Vise
Square—carpenter's try square or
    machinist's combination square
Tubing cutter, if one plans to cut a lot of small-diameter pipe
4x8-foot plywood panel or large, wood-top workbench
C-clamps, 3-inch or larger

3. Cutting and Bending

PLASTIC PIPE is manufactured in twenty-foot lengths. Shops catering to craftsmen and do-it-yourselfers will cut the pipe in half lengths or shorter. But to make furniture, we have to cut the rigid pipe into shorter lengths ourselves.

The plastic pipe we use is tough at normal temperatures. It has some spring to it and can be bent a little, but it will always return to its original straight form when released. To give it a permanent bend the plastic has to be heated to 350–400 degrees F. This is a task that takes care and lots of practice to do properly, but it can be done at home. Therefore the technique is described in detail further along in this chapter for those who want to include curved pieces in their furniture.

CUTTING AND DRILLING

Freehand When the pipe's diameter is less than ¾ inch and there is no special need for a square end, the pipe can simply be held firm against a box or bench and sawed. A slight angle on the end of the pipe that enters a fitting does no harm.

Tubing cutter A much easier way to cut small-diameter pipe is to use a tubing cutter. The desired line of cut is marked on the pipe. The cutter is positioned on the pipe, and the cutting wheel is lowered until it presses lightly against the line-of-cut mark. Then the entire cutter is rotated around the pipe. The cutting wheel is pressed a bit more firmly against the pipe. This is accomplished by turning the tool's handle. The entire device is again swung around the pipe. The cutting wheel is tightened a little more, and the tool is kept turn-

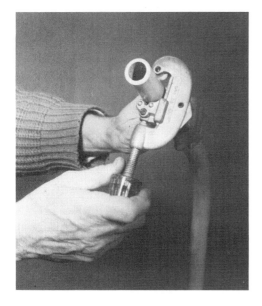

(Left) The easy and accurate way to cut plastic pipe is with a tubing cutter.

(Right) Pipe that is too large to be cut with the tubing cutter can be easily cut squarely across by using a miter box.

ing until the pipe is severed. In most instances the cut ends of the pipe will be somewhat thickened. If the pipe end will not enter the fitting, the lip or ridge on the pipe end is filed down with a file or some sandpaper.

When the pipe's diameter is more than ¾ inch a slight angle on the pipe's end can seriously affect its full entrance into the fitting. So, the cut must be made square. This is easily done by placing the pipe in a miter box and sawing away with either a backsaw or a fine-toothed crosscut saw.   *Miter box*

Any pipe that is too large in diameter to fit inside the miter box— that is, projecting above the sides of the box—can be cut square across by the following procedure: *Oversize pipe*

A piece of paper is folded down its length to form a straight

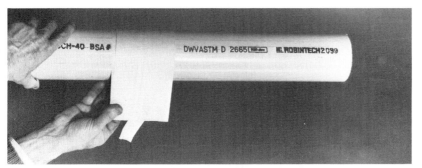

The way to cut pipe too large for your miter box is to wrap a straight-edged fold of paper around the pipe, then follow the edge with your saw. If the paper's edge is straight then it will follow a perfect, right angle path around the pipe.

edge. The paper is wrapped around the pipe so that the straight edge is continuous and in line with the desired line of cut. With a piece or two of scotch tape, the paper is fastened to the pipe. The line formed by the folded edge of the paper will be perpendicular to the pipe. Cutting along this line will cut straight across the pipe.

Shaping pipe ends   In some instances one may want to chamfer the ends of a small-diameter pipe so that it can be butted more smoothly against the side of a larger-diameter or even equal-diameter pipe.

The small pipe is placed on a flat surface, and the large-diameter pipe is held vertically against the side of the small pipe. The desired line of cut is marked with a pencil. Then, with a saw, a "V" is cut into the small-pipe end. The end of the pipe is filed down with a round file, or coarse sandpaper wrapped around a dowel, until the end conforms to the curved line that has been drawn.

Holes in pipe   Small holes are easily drilled into the sides of plastic pipe with a twist drill and a standard drill motor. A drill motor of any size will do, but if one is purchasing a motor, the ⅜-inch drill motor is recommended. Its bit speed is lower and thus it works better.

To keep the point of the twist drill from wandering, the desired hole center should be center-punched. Almost anything will do for a center punch, even a nail.

Speedbor bits can make holes larger than those possible with

Wrap cardboard around your pipe when you place it in your vise. Use a very light pressure on the Speedbor bit once its point has dug it, and then hold the drill motor as steady as you can.

the twist bits that fit the drill motor. Speedbors are designed for use with small drill motors to cut through wood. No special technique is required to use these bits on plastic pipe, except a little caution. The pipe is fastened in a vise or placed on the floor; the person drilling stands on the pipe, applying a very gentle pressure—and ready for the bit to jam when the hole is almost completely drilled through. When the bit does jam, the driller backs off and then brings the bit slowly forward—into the plastic—again.

BENDING

Plastic pipe will hold a bend permanently only when it has been heated to 350 degrees F. This temperature must be reached or slightly exceeded by the entire mass of plastic. Plastic has a "memory." At lower than 350 degrees, the plastic will give but will "remember" its former shape and may gradually return to that shape.

If the temperature is exceeded the plastic will suddenly soften and give way completely. This is why it is difficult to bend plastic pipe at home. With too low a temperature the pipe is difficult to bend and returns to its original shape. Too high a temperature and the pipe collapses.

Preparing the guide

On a wooden-top workbench or on a sheet of plywood placed on the floor, the desired curve is drawn. It is then outlined with blocks of wood, and care is taken to round the edges of the blocks to make a smooth-walled guide.

Here the desired curve has been chalked on the work board or bench top. Now, wood guides are nailed to the board. Note that the guides stand clear of the chalk line so that the pipe will lie directly on the line.

Preparing the pipe   A length of rope is laid down the length of the desired curve. The desired ends of the curve are marked on the rope. The rope is straightened. Now a mark-to-mark measurement is made; this gives the exact length of pipe needed to go around the bend. (There is a formula by which this extra length can be computed, but the above method is easier.) The pipe is cut to the measured length. A few extra inches will do no harm. One end of the pipe is sealed with a cap and held in place with screws. (Fastening caps and similar fittings are covered in the following chapter.) The other end is covered with a cap. The screws are installed, then removed, along with the cap. They should be kept handy, along with the screwdriver.

Now a metal baking tin is filled with more than enough clean sand to fill the pipe. Tin and sand are placed in the oven, with thermostat set to 375 degrees F. The sand is given an hour or two to heat thoroughly. While it is heating, the oven should be opened and a spoon or similar instrument run through the sand a few times. This is done to loosen the sand and allow the moisture to escape more readily.

Preparing to pour   Before the sand is heated, a metal funnel is prepared by cutting off a portion of the tin's lower end, so that the hole, through which the sand will be poured, is as large as possible; the sand should flow quickly into the pipe. With bricks or blocks of wood, some sort of guide is made, to hold the pipe in a vertical position while the sand is being poured. A pair of heavy cotton gloves is also needed—heavy enough to protect the hands from the heat.

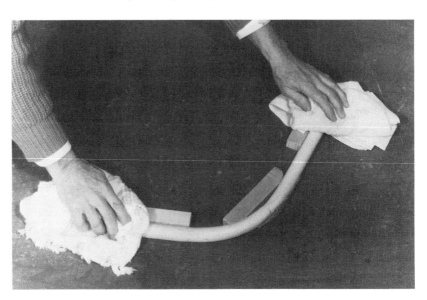

The pipe, heated by hot sand enclosed within, is now slowly and carefully bent to follow the chalked curve.

The funnel is placed in the open end of the upended pipe, and the *Pouring* sand is poured into the pipe until it is full, at which time the pipe *and bending* end is covered with the waiting cap. The cap is fastened with the screws. Then the pipe is lifted gently and placed in the guide, with hand pressure applied on the ends of the pipe to produce the bend. If the pipe does not give immediately, wait; the sand will do its job in a few minutes. Once the pipe is bent or curved as desired, cooling can be hastened by sloshing water over the pipe.

The heating and bending process is essentially simple, but perfect or even near-perfect results are difficult to achieve. The beginner should not be surprised if a few pieces of pipe are wasted in the process of trying to make satisfactory bends.

Long cracks and the like can be repaired by cleaning the crack **REPAIRS** and filling it with cement. Then the parts are held together tightly with any kind of clamp or weights.

Short breaks—such as those directly across a pipe—cannot be repaired this way. The cement cannot be trusted to hold well enough. Such breaks are repaired with a slip fitting. This is a short length of pipe without internal stops or obstructions. The break is separated. The fitting is slipped over one end of the break. The area around the break is cleaned with steel wool or sandpaper. Then the area is covered with cement. The slip fitting is slid down over the cement. When the cement hardens completely—this takes two hours at room temperature—the job is done.

4. Joints

THERE ARE any number of ways by which rigid PVC or CPVC pipe can be joined to itself, and to panels of wood, plastic, and glass. Many of these ways will be covered in the following pages. All of the joint types will not be used in the projects that comprise the second half of this book. But all the reasonably useful and practical joints are described here, should they be needed in a reader's special projects and designs.

FITTED JOINTS   To simplify discussion in this book, joints formed between pieces of pipe by means of a fitting of one kind or another are designated fitted joints.

Dry-fitted joints   Very simply, the end of the pipe is slipped into the fitting as far as it will go. Nothing more is done. In most instances there is an interference fit between pipe and fitting. The pipe is snug. This is the design tolerance. If the pipe end is loose, another fitting or another section of pipe should be tried. Neither the fitting nor the pipe is ever exactly on size. Instead it is manufactured to a tolerance, which means the pipe and fitting may be a little larger or smaller than the specified dimension. This is normal. Thus, with an undersize pipe and an oversize fitting the joint will be "sloppy"—a machinist's term for a loose fit. If pipe and fitting cannot be matched satisfactorily, the fitting should be exchanged.

When and where the pressure on the dry joint is in line with the fitting, the pressure will hold the joint together. In such cases nothing more need be done to the joint.

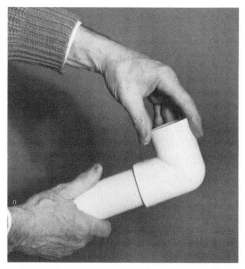

A dry fitted joint. It holds together by virtue of the friction between the pipe end and the fitting. In many instances, nothing more need be done than insert the pipe into the fitting.

When the pressure or load is such as to pull the pipe out of the fitting, or to rotate the fitting on the pipe end when this is not desired, the fitting can be firmly and permanently locked to the pipe with two self-tapping metal screws driven through the fitting and into the pipe. Table 1 gives screw types and sizes, and drill sizes that may be used. Note that the hole through the fitting is a clearance hole, meaning it is larger than the body of the screw. The hole into the pipe is smaller than the body of the screw. This allows the screw to be forced into the pipe and thus cut its own threads.

Screw-fastened joints

If there is uncertainty as to which joints one wishes to leave dry and which one wants to fasten with screws, the piece of furniture need simply be assembled; then, the need—if any—for screw-fastened joints will become obvious.

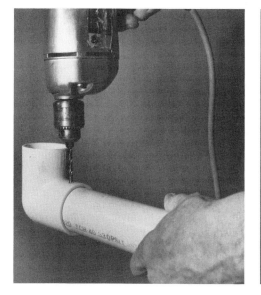
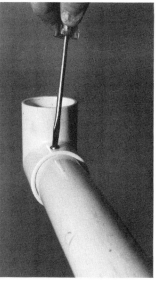

To make a screw-fastened joint.

(Left) Assemble the joint. Drill a pilot hole through the fitting and the pipe. Then drill a clearance hole through the fitting alone.

(Right) Drive a sheet metal screw through the fitting and into the pipe.

Permanent joints The pipe-to-fitting joints that will be assembled in the process of making pipe furniture are designed to carry and hold water. To keep the joints from leaking, the pipe is "welded" to the fitting with cement. The word "welded" is not an exaggeration. Once properly cemented, the joint will not only hold water under pressure but will not come apart. In fact, an error in cementing a pipe-fitting joint makes it necessary to discard the pipe and fitting. (A portion of the pipe can be saved by cutting the fitting off.) Thus, one must be certain of the joint and its rotation—relation of one part to another—before cementing the pieces fast.

SCREW AND DRILL SIZE TABLE

For sheet metal screws in plastic pipe

Screw size*	Pilot drill size	Clearance drill size[†]
#6	7/64 inch	9/64 inch
#8	1/8	11/64
#10	5/32	3/16
#12	11/64	7/32

To start, the pipe end is tried in the fitting; it can be a little loose, as the cement will make the joint tight. The joint or joints are assembled dry. It is important to make certain that all the joints and parts are orthogonal—meaning that the chair legs or table legs or whatever are perpendicular to the objects they hold up. Next, a pencil mark is made on the fitting and on the adjoining pipe so that the joint can be reassembled properly after disassembly. If there is uncertainty that some fitting-to-pipe rotation may take place during reassembly and cementing, each joint should be locked with a single, temporary screw. When reassembling, it is necessary only to make certain that the screw lines up with the hole.

The pipe end is removed from the fitting. With sandpaper, steel wool, or cement "primer," the shine is removed from the pipe's end surface for the distance it enters the fitting. One smooth, even layer of cement is applied to the pipe end; this layer should be made just as wide as the distance the pipe enters the fitting. The pipe end is slipped into the fitting, which is held fast. The pipe end is given a quarter turn or so, bringing it to rest with its guide mark aligned with the guide mark on the fitting, or with the screw holes in line with one another. There's no need to fuss: just one fraction-turn or a little more is made before stopping. In about

* Screw size is given as a number. Screw length has no bearing on screw size.
[†] Clearance drill sizes may be larger if desired.

To make a permanent joint

(Left) Assemble the joint. If the rotational position of the fitting in relation to the pipe is important, mark the desired position of the fitting against the pipe.

(Right) Remove the shine from the end of the pipe with steel wool or sandpaper.

(Left) Apply solvent cement to the end of the pipe.

(Right) Quickly slip the fitting over the pipe end and give the fitting a fractional turn and bring it into the desired position as indicated by the marks you have made.

thirty seconds the cement will set and the joint will be almost permanent. In two hours at 70 degrees F it will be permanent.

For best results the cement and the pipe should be at about 70 degrees F or higher. At lower temperatures cement action slows down. If the cement is so cold as to be ropy, it should be heated up by setting the closed can in hot water for a few minutes. If the cement is not cold but still thick and ropy, a little cement thinner should be added.

Note that PVC cement is to be used for PVC pipe, and CPVC cement for CPVC pipe. Note too that the cement and especially the thinners and primers have a horrible, noxious stink. One must be certain to open all the windows when opening any of these cans.

For maximum portability and storage it is obvious that it is best not to cement any of the joints. This, of course, is not always possible. On many of the designs it will be necessary to cement several if not all the joints. Assuming the option to let a large number of joints remain dry, it should be remembered that too many dry joints make it difficult to reassemble the furniture. Not that it is difficult to insert a pipe into a fitting, but it is confusing when there are lots of pieces of pipe and lots of joints and fittings.

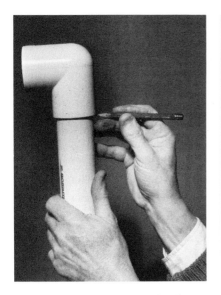

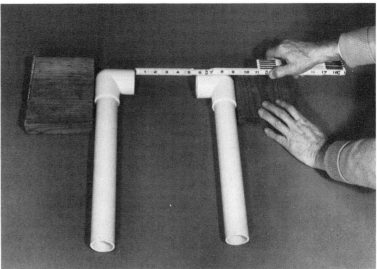

To measure pipe insertion depth, insert the pipe into the fitting, mark the edge of the fitting on the side of the pipe. Remove the pipe. Measure from your mark to the end of the pipe.

To determine necessary pipe length, position the two fittings and associated pipe the desired distance apart on your work bench. Measure the distance between the facing fitting ends. To this dimension add the two insertion depths to get the overall length of the necessary pipe.

Measuring pipe insertion depth   With the exception of the slip fitting, a pipe will enter a fitting for a distance that is close to the pipe's size—that is to say, its internal diameter. In some instances this distance will be a little more than the pipe's I.D., in some a little less. How can one be certain of this dimension plus the space occupied by the balance of the fitting? Measure the pipe insertion depth then place the two fittings on the floor or workbench—the exact desired distance apart. Then the distance from fitting end to fitting end is measured. If this distance is, for example, two feet and it is known that the pipe insertion depth at each fitting is two inches, a pipe two feet four inches long is needed. If there is no objection to extra cutting and one wants to be certain, the pipe can be cut a little long, then tried and corrected as needed.

Compression joints   Compression fittings in both metal and plastic are manufactured for the plumbing trade, mainly for use in drainpipe assemblies. We mention them here because they can be tightened and loosened by hand-turning a large, knurled nut. In some designs the pipe end can be inserted into the fitting a limited distance and no more. In other compression-joint fittings the pipe can be slipped through the fitting and into the following pipe (assuming its diameter is large enough) any distance. This makes the fitting suitable for varying the length of a portion of the furniture. For example, to make a table lamp with a variable-height arm, a compression fitting would be used in the center-post assembly. To vary the

 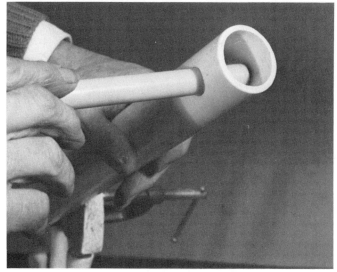

Typical compression joint made by simply using a compression fitting. Rotating the large knob tightens and loosens the joint.

Simple inserted joint. Pipe end can be fastened in position a number of ways or left as is.

braces holding the backrest of a beach chair or chaise so that the angle of the backrest could be adjusted to suit, a compression fitting in each brace would do the trick.

Whereas fitted joints are always made with factory-produced fittings, non-fitted joints betwen pipes are made without fittings. The general differences in the resulting joints are appearance, size (fitted joints are larger), cost (non-fitted joints are cheaper), and strength (usually, fitted joints are stronger).

NON-FITTED PIPE JOINTS

A hole is drilled through one side of one pipe, which of course must be the larger-diameter pipe. The end of the smaller pipe is slipped into the hole. This may sound useless here, but it is not. Let us say that someone wants to provide a backrest consisting of a number of horizontal or vertical lengths of small-diameter pipe, positioned fairly closely together. Not only would the cost of a T-fitting for each end of each pipe bring the cost way up, but the fittings themselves would not permit spacing the pipes closely. By placing two T-fittings end to end this will immediately become obvious.

Inserted joints

The pipe ends are not cemented or otherwise fastened in their holes. A little to-and-fro motion does no harm and only takes place when the furniture is moved.

The end of one pipe is chamfered to fit snugly up against the side of another pipe. The pipe with the chamfered end can be as large or even a little larger than the pipe to which side it is fastened—

End-to-side joints

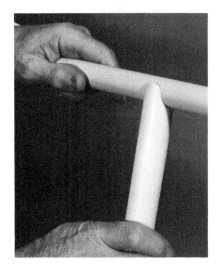
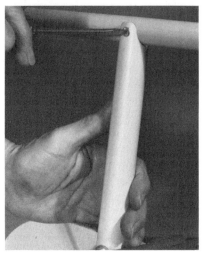

(Left) End-to-side joint made by simply cementing chamfered end of pipe to side of second pipe.

(Right) End-to-side joint made stronger by screw fastening end pipe to side pipe.

but *not* smaller than ⅔ the diameter of the "side" pipe. There are three ways in which these joints are usually made.

One, the end of the pipe is simply chamfered. A little cement is applied and pressed into place. Alone, this joint won't hold beans. It should be used only when and where the other end of the chamfered pipe is also chamfered and locked in place against another pipe. Even this arrangement is not recommended where pressure is expected on the joint. But it will do for ornamentation. If the second joint on the chamfered pipe is a fitted joint, or is held by a screw in some strong fashion, some weight can be applied safely to the glued joint, but not much.

Two, chamfered pipe, much larger in diameter than the side pipe, is used. The ends of the chamfer are allowed to overlap the side pipe. The chamfer ends are fastened to the side pipe with screws.

Three, the pipe end is chamfered as described. A long block of wood is cemented inside the chafered pipe-end, the top of the wood to be farther in than the chamfer. Holes are drilled through the side pipe. The chamfered pipe is positioned against the side pipe. Now a screw is driven through the side pipe and into the block of wood.

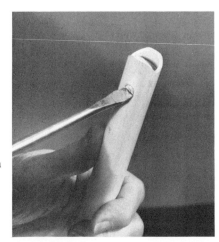

Another way to screw-fasten an end-to-side joint. A short dowel is fastened with a screw within the end of the "end" pipe. Then a long wood screw is driven through the side pipe and into the end of the dowel.

A half-fitted joint. As can be seen, half of the T has been cut away. Fitting just rests on side pipe. Joint is useful only where pressure is downward against the side pipe. Note that "stop" within fitting has to be filed down first.

Half-fitted joints

These are pipe-to-pipe joints made by using a portion of a fitting between them. For example, a chaise is being made. It has two long sides to which a number of crossbars must be fastened for supports. If T-fittings are used to hold and position the crossbars, it will be necessary to cut the long pipes forming the sides into a number of short pieces. Not only is this work, but it will weaken the chaise to some extent.

On the other hand, if T-fittings are used with a portion of the T cut away, the T-fitting can simply be pressed down onto the side bars. Since the load is down, there is no need for the under half of the fitting. Note that all the pipe fittings have a "stop," which is a slightly raised central, inner area that has to be filed down when something like this is done. The function of the stop is literally to stop the inserted pipes from going too far into the fitting. (Only the slip coupling does not have a stop.)

PANEL-TO-PIPE JOINTS

In some instances—coffee tables for example—the panel can simply be laid in place. The weight of the panel holds it in place. In other instances the panel must be fastened to the pipe frame in one way or another. Some of the more frequently used panel-to-pipe joints are now discussed.

Lay-on joints

These are the simplest and easiest. The panel rests on top of the pipe. Holes drilled up through the pipe permit fastening the panel to the pipe with screws. If desired, a long screw can be used. Or an oversize hole can be drilled through one wall of the pipe, and a short screw can then be run into the panel through a clearance hole.

The disadvantage of this type of joint is that the edges of the panel are visible; the exposed edges may or may not be considered attractive. If not, there are any number of standard, panel-edge treatments that can be used. One is simply to sand the edge

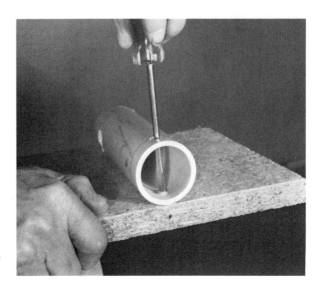

A lay-on joint. One normal clearance hole and a second, over-size clearance hole have been drilled through the pipe. Now a screw is being driven through the pipe and into the piece of chipboard. When the assembly is turned over, the screw and the hole in the pipe will be out of sight.

as smooth as possible and forget it. Another is to glue a strip of edging veneer to the edge of the panel. Still another is to glaze the edge; this means the edge is first given a thinned coat of paint, sanded, and then varnished. The paint tends to hide the wood grain to some degree.

Edge-to-pipe joints   The panel is positioned alongside the pipe. For best appearance, the edge of the panel is chamfered—even a shallow groove here helps considerably. Holes are drilled through the pipe and screws are driven through the holes and into the panel. Again, one has the choice of using a long screw or drilling an oversized hole through one wall of the pipe and then a clearance hole through the second wall. This allows the use of short screws, but leaves a hole visible in the pipe wall.

(Left) An edge-to-point joint. A normal clearance hole and a second, over-size clearance hole have been drilled through the pipe. Now a screw is being driven into the edge of the chipboard. In this case the edge has been chamfered somewhat to make for a close fit.

(Right) Another type of edge-to-pipe joint. In this version the edge of the chipboard fits into a slot cut into the side of the pipe.

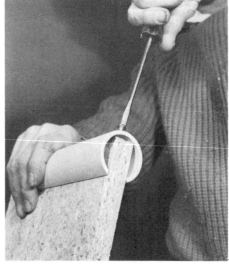

Another method of making an edge-to-pipe joint consists of cutting a wide slot down the length of the pipe. The panel is slipped into the slot. Screws through the pipe hold in place. This makes for a beautiful, neat, and strong joint. Unfortunately, the slot is difficult to cut with a handsaw on pipe much more than a foot in length. However, with a table saw and a guide, it is a snap. It might be worthwhile to look for a lumber yard that has a table saw and will make the cuts for a small fee.

The frame is first constructed and assembled. It is then disassembled and the slots are cut in the pipe. Now the frame is reassembled, with the panels simultaneously slipped into place— after some of the panel corners and other areas where the panels strike the fittings have been cut away.

Panels should be used that are large enough not to slip sideways and out of one slot. Or, some wood screws can be fastened to each panel side so that the panel cannot move and slip out of place. In other words, the screws in the panel edges act as center spacers. The slots are, of course, just a bit wider than the thickness of the panels, and the slots run the length of each pipe.

Previous panel-to-pipe joinery had the panel edge parallel to and in line with the length of the pipe. The cross-pipe joint is used when the edge of the panel crosses the length of the pipe. *Cross-pipe joint*

This joint can be made by using a metal bracket screwed fast to the pipe and also to the panel's underside. This is not too difficult, using a ⅛-inch by 1-inch strip of aluminum, cut and bent to shape. The advantage of the arrangement is that the pipe stands proud of the panel, giving full use of the panel's surface for storage and other purposes.

As an alternative, a slot can be cut across the pipe and the edge of the panel slid into the slot. Or the corner of the panel can be cut off and the truncated corner slid into the slot. In either ar-

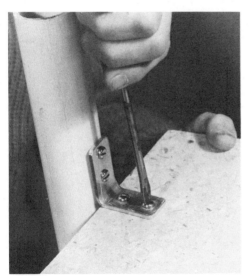

A cross-pipe joint. This type is made by fastening the chipboard to the pipe with a small metal angle. When completed, the assembly is turned over, hiding the screws and the angle.

An alternative cross-pipe joint.

(Left) The thickness of the board or panel to be supported is laid out on the pipe. (Right) Two parallel saw cuts are made in the pipe. The cuts may be as deep as half the diameter of the pipe, but no more. Spacing between the cuts should be no more than the thickness of the panel.

(Left) A small hole is drilled through the pipe at the bottom of each saw cut. (Right) A coping saw is used to connect the two drilled holes.

A section of the pipe can now be removed.

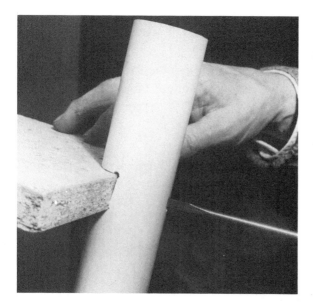

(Left) The edge of the panel, in this case a chipboard panel, is slipped into the slot. A screw driven through the pipe and into the panel edge holds it firmly in place. (Right) Here we are looking into the pipe. In this example, the cut-off corner of the panel has been placed within the pipe and is being fastened in place with a screw.

rangement, a screw is then driven through a hole in the pipe and into the panel edge. When fairly large-diameter pipe is used and the fit between the panel and slot is tight, the joint is not only strong so far as vertical loading is concerned, but is also fairly rigid. Put another way, this corner-in-the pipe arrangement enables fairly stable self-supporting shelves (such as an open book case) to be made with just four lengths of pipe and shelves.

TERMINATIONS The factory ends of the plastic pipe we use are smooth and burr free. After sawing, the pipe end usually has a few burrs and hairs. These can be removed with a file. If the pipe is going to stand vertically on the grass or on a concrete or stone patio, nothing more need be done to it. If the pipe is to stand on a good wood floor or a rug, it is best to terminate the pipe end with a pipe cap. This can be fastened in place with cement or a screw.

Should one want the pipe end to be a little "hokey," the end can be terminated with a flange. This is a sort of on-edge flat-ring type of fitting. It can be cemented or screwed in place.

The upper ends of the pipe that do not terminate in fittings can be similarly treated.

REINFORCEMENT As stated previously, plastic pipe can carry a considerable compressive load. That is to say, when the pipe is in a vertical position. But it is weak when used and loaded in a horizontal position, which of course produces a tensile load. Whether for a specific design purpose or simply to save money by using smaller-diameter pipe than suggested, the same strength or even more can be achieved by reinforcing the pipe. There are several ways to do this.

Concrete reinforcement After being cut to length, or even after being almost completely assembled, one end of the pipe is blocked with a wad of wet paper. The pipe is then stood on end and filled with wet cement. Standard construction cement is mixed with two parts sand, and sufficient water is added to make a soup, after which, with the aid of a funnel, the pipe is filled with the mixture. If the funnel end is cut short so that the hole there is larger than usual, the cement will flow more freely. The pipe should be shaken and otherwise vibrated, still in a vertical position, while the mix continues to be poured into the pipe until the mix itself appears at the top of the pipe. After a few minutes the cement will settle a little farther down and more water will come to the top. More cement is now added. The pipe does not have to be completely filled with cement, but as much as possible should be poured in.

The filled pipe should stand in a vertical positon—or the open end should be plugged—and nothing more done than move the pipe out of the way for a week. The cement takes this long to harden properly. Filled with hardened cement this way, the reinforced pipe is as strong—actually as stiff—as a pipe one and a half to two times its diameter.

When the diameter of the pipe permits their addition, small

This pipe is being reinforced with cement. The bottom of the pipe is plugged with wet paper. The cement is poured into the pipe and permitted to settle. Then the water that will come to the top is poured off and replaced with more cement. To use steel to reinforce the pipe, position the steel within the pipe, then pour the cement around it.

stones can be added to the cement to make it concrete, which is stronger than cement alone.

In many instances it may not be necessary to reinforce more than a short section of the pipe. For example, one may want to reinforce only the angle in the frame of a chaise—where the bend portion turns up to form the supportive back. For this, one end of the angled pipe is blocked with a wad of wet paper. A bent iron rod is forced into the angled portion of the pipe. Then, to lock the metal in place, the remaining space is filled with wet cement as suggested. *Metal and concrete reinforcement*

Note that the pouring of cement into a narrow pipe results in a considerable amount of slopping about, so the job should either be done outdoors, or the work-area floor covered with plenty of old newspapers.

A suitable length of hardwood having a square or nearly square cross section is selected. Then the corners of the piece of wood are removed. The wood is coated with wet soap and forced into *Wood reinforcement*

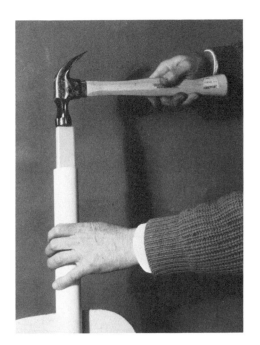

A length of wood may be driven into a pipe to stiffen it. You want a snug fit here, but don't force the wood or you may pull the pipe out of round and the fittings won't go on.

the length of pipe. The soap acts merely as a lubricant. Note that together, the wood and the pipe are stronger by far than the total of their individual strengths. (To learn how much the wood has stiffened the pipe, just try bending it.)

5. Design

NO MATTER HOW MANY construction projects may be illustrated in this or any book, and no matter how large the book may be, no single book, or even a set of books, can possibly include every type, size, and kind of plastic pipe furniture that can be constructed. That is one reason for this chapter on design: to free the reader from the limitations imposed by the relatively few examples of plastic-pipe furniture craft presented herein. Another reason—just as important—is simply that it is fun to plan and design one's own plastic-pipe furniture.

Asked where they get their ideas, designers will probably reply with the "fish eye." A design person is creative, and creativity is just there, a God-given gift, something one is blessed with at birth. Creativity cannot be explained; explanation should not even be attempted. To fool with the creative process is to destroy it. This is, of course, pure droppings from the cowshed. No brain produces ideas of any kind of and from itself. Like a computer, a brain must be fed data to produce results. Design computers require design input.

Consciously or unconsciously, a designer in any field whatsoever will visually examine what has been done before, what has been accomplished in related fields, and will churn it all together, hopefully to produce what is more than a variation on a theme.

Craftspeople wishing to develop new and novel furniture ideas of their own should visit furniture showrooms to see what is being done in wood, metal, and plastic by contemporary designers and manufacturers. Nor should anyone hesitate to imitate. All

SOURCE OF IDEAS

47

How a design for a tea chart might evolve.

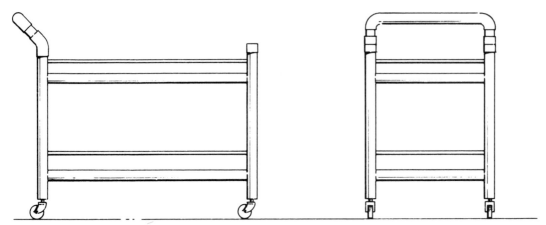

Side and end views sketched of the proposed cart.

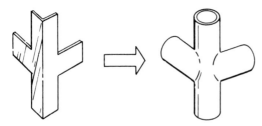

Corner joint could be made of a right-angle cross fitting. (Couldn't find one; idea dropped.)

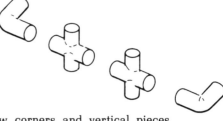

How corners and vertical pieces might be joined: 90 degree angles, plus two straight Tees. (Dropped because vertical pieces would be several inches in from sides of cart.)

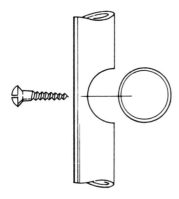

A groove could be cut in the vertical pieces. Supporting frame could be slipped in and fastened with a screw. (Dropped because once again vertical pieces would be too far away from sides of cart.)

Supposing a circular section was cut from a 90 degree angle? That would put vertical piece right on the side and corner of the supporting frame.

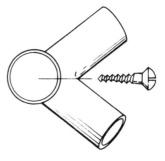

This is how the arrangement would work. A secondary advantage would be the minimum number of fittings required.

This is one way the glass panes could be supported by the frame. (Dropped; slot cut is too difficult without power tools.)

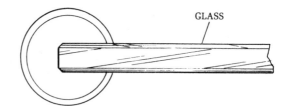

GLASS

Glass panes or panels could be replaced by boards and held in place with screws. (Dropped because an attractive board 15 or so inches wide would have to be cut from a 4 × 8-foot panel, which would be very expensive as you would have to purchase the entire panel. It was therefore decided to simply lay the panels of glass on top of the supporting frames.)

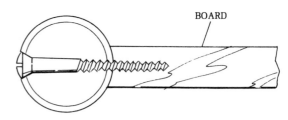

BOARD

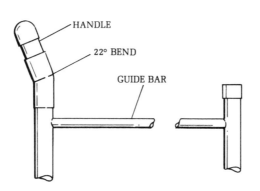

HANDLE

22° BEND

GUIDE BAR

The easiest way to provide guard rails or bars would be to use thin pipe and slip the pipe ends into holes in the vertical pieces.

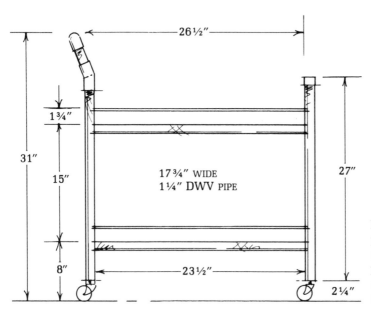

26½"

1¾"

31"

15"

17¾" WIDE
1¼" DWV PIPE

27"

8"

23½"

2¼"

Rough sketch and dimensions of proposed tea cart. Overall width is 17¾ inches, and 1¼-inch DWV pipe was selected. This is the tea cart that is described and actually constructed in Chapter 10.

designers do. (An examination of women's fashions will reveal that they repeat themselves every twenty years or so.) If in a lifetime of designing a design person comes up with something truly original, he or she is in the genius class, and a genius can hardly ever be found. So nobody should hesitate to copy—but everybody should try to add a little of their own.

START WITH A SKETCH The very beginning should be a rough drawing or a sketch of the furniture one would like to construct. The sketch needn't be at an angle to the viewer. Although this helps, simple frontal and side views are enough.

For those who don't want to trouble to measure all lines, drawings can be made on graph paper, with so many boxes assigned to the foot. In this way the proportions of the various parts of a design can be quickly determined.

Proportions Since, perforce, we are working with simple angles, limited by their availability, and straight pipe, we can control or vary nothing but overall size and the ratio of one part to another—that is to say, the proportions of the design. Although this may not appear to be much, the increase or reduction of, say, the height or width of a chair's back can greatly alter its appearance. Thus, so much pipe for this part and so much for that part, on the basis of eliminating waste, cannot be allowed. To use every inch of pipe purchased is the height of economy, but if the resulting furniture does not look attractive, everything has been wasted.

Make a model To get a better preview of a completed design than what a simple sketch can provide, a model of the design should be made. A model is easily made from wooden matchsticks and Duco cement. A razor is used to cut the sticks. A flat, partial assembly of the model is made on wax paper. Then the parts are assembled. When the model is completed, its appearance can be better appreciated if the eye is brought down to its level.

Scale the model Continuing on the importance of proportions, if the model looks good, its parts should be scaled. In other words, each part must be measured carefully. Thus, if one part is actually two inches and another is one-and-a-half inches, the same relationship should be held when working full size. The smaller part should be 75 per cent of the larger part (1.5 divided by 2). If full-size pipe construction is not held to the same proportions admired in the model, the entire effort is for naught.

DIMENSIONS There are three constraints in determining the actual dimensions of projects and their various parts. They are as follows:

The basic constraint, of course is the human body. Chairs, tables, *Bodies* and other articles of furniture must be suited to the average *and things* body's needs. If not, the user of this furniture will be uncomfortable. Seat heights and the like are given in the accompanying illustration.

When the human frame is not involved, as is the case with coffee tables, bookcases, and the like, the shape and weight of whatever is to be placed on or in these articles must be considered.

The second constraint on the design may be imposed by prefab- *Prefabricated* ricated parts, such as pads, cushions, glass, and wood panels that *components* the pipe frame will support or otherwise utilize. For example, there is little sense to making a seat bottom two and a half feet wide when cushions and pads are not normally manufactured in this width. The same would be true of plate glass, marble slabs, and even wood and plastic panels. If it is necessary to have glass or marble cut and polished (edges) to fit a construction, one is certainly going to pay more for these parts—plus the loss of time waiting for the work to be accomplished.

While it is true that wood and plastic panels are easily cut, selecting the wrong dimension can be wasteful. For example, wood panels are normally four by eight feet in size. Should one decide to use the panel in one-foot-sixteen-inch or two-foot-wide strips, there would be no waste; any other strip widths and there would be leftover strips, which, unless needed, would be a costly waste.

The third constraint on design is load, meaning the load or stress *Load* that will be placed on what is built. Load presents no problem if the suggestions in the accompanying illustration—or the pipe diameters used in the projects—are followed.

However, for those who wish to go off on their own completely, or to go to a smaller-diameter pipe to save money, thought should be given to the following.

The compressive strength of plastic pipe is high; therefore, except for stiffness, there is no need to worry about a vertical member of a design. Held vertically, plastic pipe will carry just about any load one cares to place on it. It's the horizontal and near-horizontal that requires thought.

A horizontal load on a length of pipe, meaning a tensile load, tends to bend the pipe and break it. In addition, when this piece of pipe is subjected to the load and exposed to a hot sun for a long time, the pipe may sag and take on a permanent bend. Obviously, it requires a lot more pressure actually to break a piece of pipe than to cause it to sag when hot. This means that if one never plans to expose the plastic furniture to a hot sun, the next diameter smaller than suggested can be used, without problems.

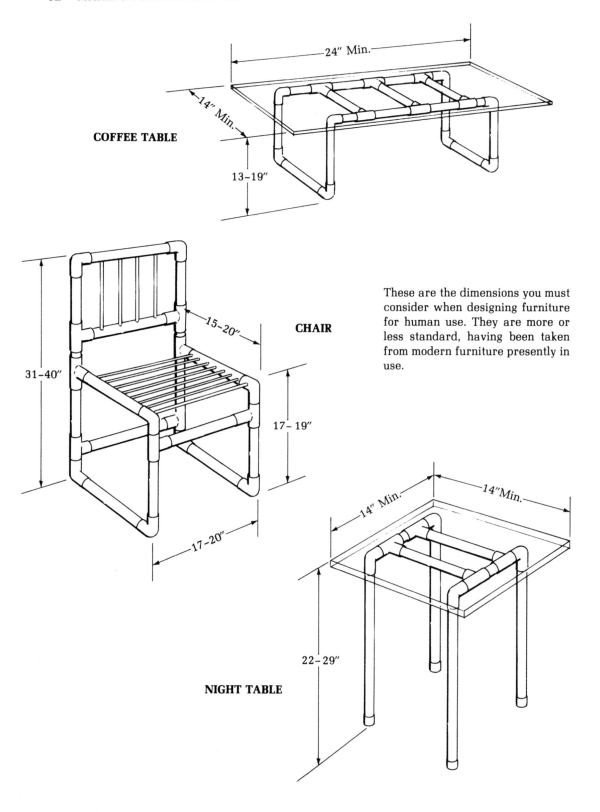

COFFEE TABLE

24″ Min.

14″ Min.

13–19″

CHAIR

31–40″

15–20″

17–19″

17–20″

These are the dimensions you must consider when designing furniture for human use. They are more or less standard, having been taken from modern furniture presently in use.

NIGHT TABLE

14″ Min.

14″ Min.

22–29″

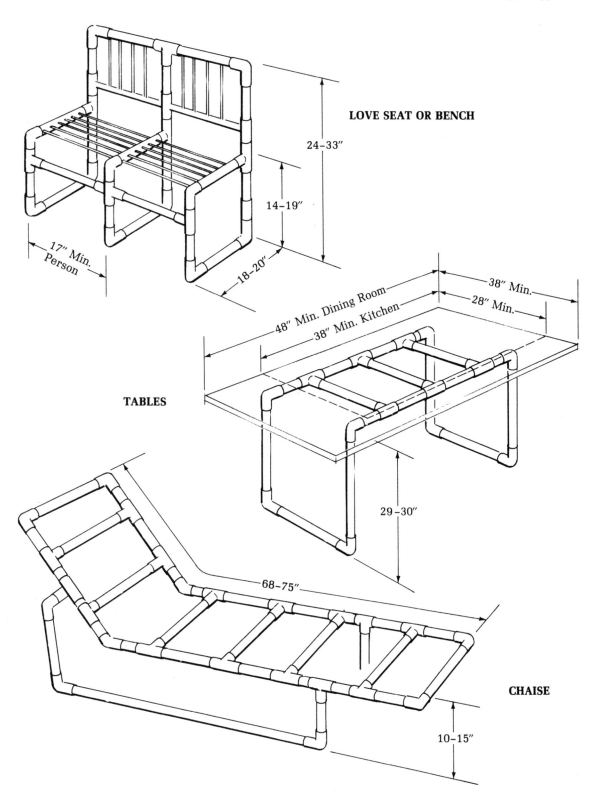

LOVE SEAT OR BENCH

24–33″

14–19″

17″ Min.
Person

18–20″

38″ Min.

28″ Min.

48″ Min. Dining Room

38″ Min. Kitchen

TABLES

29–30″

68–75″

CHAISE

10–15″

Assume that a craftsperson wants to cut down on pipe diameter but is uncertain whether or not the sun in his or her area will be too hot, or whether the pipe will be subjected to direct sunlight for long periods. The following will be useful. The furniture is constructed, but screws are used for the joints. Then it is a matter of "wait and see." If the pipe sags—and it will not be more than a gentle curve unless very small-diameter pipe has been used—the furniture should be disassembled, the bent pipe given half a turn, and another summer spent waiting. Then, when the pipe has sagged straight, it should be reinforced as suggested in chapter 4.

We are not going to actually compute the load on a piece of pipe. We are just going to explain how the load may be evaluated.

Assume that two strong boxes have been placed on the floor and separated by exactly one foot. If a pipe is placed across the tops of the boxes and one presses down in the middle of the pipe, a load is being placed on one foot of the pipe. The overall length of the pipe does not matter. If the boxes are spread until they are two feet apart, the load is on a two-foot-long pipe. It is the distance between the pipe supports—nothing else—that is considered.

If a chaise with two side bars that carry the load is constructed, computations must be based on the fact that each pipe carries half the total load.

To judge for oneself just how much a pipe of a particular diameter will bend under load when stretched over a particular span, one should place the pipe on two supports the desired distance apart and press down on its center with all one's weight.

SUPPORTING PANELS AND PADS   Since the pipe that is to be used for the frames will be at least 3/4 inch in size and connected by fittings, the total diameter of the pipe and fitting will be at least 1 3/8 inches. Thus a panel placed on top of the pipe will be at least 9/16 inch higher than a panel positioned with its top surface in line with the center of the pipe. At the same time the panel resting on the pipe frame has to be larger than the panel positioned within the frame. And the way the panel within the frame is to be supported will also affect its required size. If the panel is to be fastened by screws, it must fit between the sides of the pipe frame. If the panel is to fit into slots in the pipe, then the panel obviously must be larger.

All these design decisions must be made and the necessary accommodating dimensions calculated prior to actual construction. Craftspeople who don't start knowing all their dimensions stand a good chance of ending up cutting and wasting time and material.

6. Construction Tips

THIS CHAPTER includes everything possibly useful to the reader that the authors know about making plastic-pipe furniture; the information cannot be fitted neatly into any of the other chapters.

Plastic pipe and pipe fittings can be found in some hardward shops, some handyman shops, and most professional plumbing supply shops. The prices at the pro shops are somewhat lower, and the stock carried is considerably larger than can be found elsewhere. At the same time the countermen may be less than interested in discussing a construction project; on learning what a purchaser wants they will simply rush back into the stockrooms to fetch it. But the buyer shouldn't ask them to tell him what he wants or needs. Naming the part is the buyer's job, not theirs. And there are too many anxious little plumbers also on line, eager to get on with it and make their day's pay.

The handyman shops will spend time with a buyer, and will often cut pipe to less than half-lengths. These shops and hardware shops often have some plastic pipe and fittings on display; this helps determine a buyer's wants and needs. But the prices are higher.

As stated, PVC is less expensive than CVPC, and just as good for our purpose. Both come in three colors; pale gray, white, and cream. To get the desired color, it's necessary to ask for it; plumbers are not concerned with color.

To be sure of the right-size fittings, a buyer should bring along a short section of pipe, and try the pipe in the fittings before accepting them. Fittings are sometimes incorrectly marked or boxed, and it is difficult to judge their size by eye. Some pipe is marked in O.D. (outside diameter); this should be watched for carefully.

When pipe and fittings are brought home, they shouldn't be dumped on the garage or basement floor; plastic pipe and fittings will be scratched rolling about on concrete. Instead, they must be laid down on several layers of newspaper, unless they can be placed on wood or some kind of rack.

Cushions, pads, and such   As stated previously, construction should always begin with these parts on hand. For one thing, advertised dimensions often turn out to be slightly different from actual dimensions. For another, the overall size of a pad or cushion is not always its working dimensions. For example, a chair cushion may be four inches high fully fluffed, but when somebody sits on it it may flatten to merely an inch. If four inches were allowed when planning bench height, the cushion would be three inches lower than expected when a guest sat down on it. Thus the cushions must be on hand so that they can be compressed to find out what the dimension change may be.

The same holds true to some extent for a cushion's length and width. It expands a bit when compressed, but this will be true only if the cushion is fully supported by a solid, flat surface. If a number of parallel, small-diameter bars are used to support the cushion, its overall width and breadth will be reduced when it is sat upon. This is due to the cushion sagging somewhat into the spaces between the bars. A stiff cushion will not change dimensions nearly as much as a very soft, fluffy cushion. This cannot be known until the cushion is in hand and actually tried out.

Also, cushions and pads seen on displayed furniture can rarely be purchased. We don't know why, but the cushions and pads sold separately in most department and furniture stores are not those to be found on their furniture; or at least are found there so rarely as to fall into the realm of the accidental. Thus anyone who sees a particular cushion or pad on display furniture and plans on using it is likely to be sadly disappointed.

Glass and marble   The same holds true for glass and marble. A manufacturer may make a beautiful glass-topped wrought iron table. He knows the glass may break, but rarely if ever will he supply the shop with a number of replacement glass tops. Should one break his top it's generally necessary to go to a glass shop and have a new plate cut to fit.

One must literally forget about cutting and hacking until a drawn plan is in hand (assuming none of the pieces illustrated in this book will be used). "Winging it" can mean only waste and extra labor.

In the following pages the various construction projects illustrated are shown being assembled in step-by-step sequence, with all the joints involved being fastened at the same time. This is done for clarity. In actual practice it is best to cut and fit all the parts "dry"; and then, if all is well, to go back and lock the parts together by any of the suggested methods. Incidentally, if the joints are being cemented, it should be remembered that in some instances two or more joints must be made simultaneously. If, for example, three corners of a rectangle are cemented, it will not be possible to position the fourth and last corner after the first three joints have set.

*Try assembling
the project first*

All necessary parts should be assembled before any pipe is cut. Fittings must be positioned—as accurately as possible—where they will eventually be placed in relation to each other. Their separation must be measured. An attempt ought to be made at placing the cushion or panel where it is to go. No effort should be spared to see how everything is going to "shape up."

*Cut
pipe last*

Should the necessary pieces of pipe work out to be an even multiple of the uncut pipe, fine. If not, the necessary cuts should be marked with pencil. In this way, by juggling the pieces from one pipe to another it is often possible to eliminate almost all waste.

*Plan
the pipe
cuts*

There may come a time when, by shortening each piece a fraction of an inch, one can save a trip to the supply shop and perhaps end up with nineteen feet of unwanted plastic pipe. That kind of economy isn't advisable. There may be some instance when the penetration of a pipe can be reduced into a fitting without any problems. Such instances will occur when the pipe is not to carry a load, or will carry a very light load. But if the pipe does not enter fully into the fitting the joint will be weak. Certainly the joint will not hold by friction alone. It may hold with an extra screw, or a screw plus cement.

*Don't
stint on
the pipe*

The need to use cement specifically formulated for PVC or CPVC pipe has already been mentioned. Outside of this problem, there is no restriction on mixing the pipe types.
    Metal pipe can also be used with the plastic pipe if the design

*Mixing
pipe types*

calls for it. This can be done by using a transition fitting between the plastic and the metal pipe.

Bevel the When the pipe is just a fraction of an inch long, its end may be
pipe end beveled, so that it will sit more deeply in the fitting. This is generally faster and easier than cutting it shorter.

Pin the Should one want to hold one or more joints in perfect alignment
joints while examining the construction, a small-diameter hole can be drilled through the underside of the joint and pipe, and a nail slipped through the holes. If the nail is bent a little before it is inserted, it will stay. In this way one can make certain everything shapes up before cementing or drilling for screws.

Finish the When wood is used in constructions, and the plan calls for var-
wood first nishing and otherwise finishing the wood, this should be done before the piece is assembled. It is a lot easier to do so than keep the stain and varnish off the pipe after assembling the furniture.

Dimension When one of the more complicated pieces of furniture is being
the parts made, it will be somewhat difficult to keep track of each piece of pipe. The easy way is to write the length of the pipe on each piece, which permits quick identification. To help reassemble a finished piece after it has been taken apart for transportation or storage, each pipe and adjoining fitting should be lettered or numbered.

Cleaning As stated previously, one has the option of leaving or removing the red, blue, or black printing on the side of the pipe. Some craftspeople clean their pipe as soon as they bring it home. This craftsperson prefers to complete the piece before cleaning it and then cementing any parts. For one thing, the printing can very often be turned out of sight, thus saving a little effort. Further, it is difficult to focus on a shiny white pipe. This is why printing is seen on some of the pieces during construction.

Tolerances Pipe and fittings are manufactured to a tolerance, which means that pipe and fitting dimensions are not exact but always plus or minus the specified dimension. In other words a little dimensional error, i.e., the tolerance, is permitted.

To us that means that some pipes will be very tight in their fittings, and some will be very loose. For a dry-fit job or a good cement job a snug fit is needed. An overly tight fit prevents the cement from entering.

So, to get the proper fit, the fittings should be switched around. But if the fit can't be achieved, if it's so tight that the pipe won't go into the fitting without a hammer, or if the pipe is so loose that it can be tilted within the fitting, *the pipe or fitting should be returned.* A plumber wouldn't accept out-of-tolerance pipes and fittings; why should a craftsperson?

Sometimes it will be easy to assemble a dry joint, but that same joint will be difficult to break apart. Here, the pipe might be held in one hand and the fitting banged lightly with another piece of pipe or a hammer. The pipe might be freed with a pair of large gas pliers. Doing so may mark the pipe, but the mark can always be sandpapered away.

Breaking the joints

PART 2

CONSTRUCTION PROJECTS

The articles of furniture illustrated and discussed on the following pages have been constructed by the authors. If a reader wishes, all he or she needs to do is follow their lead. Dimensions, lists of materials, and procedures have all been worked out. If readers prefer to go off on their own pipe-furniture-building kick, that's fine—it is easy enough to design one's own.

PARTS LIST/COFFEE TABLE

Glass   *30-inch diameter, ¼-inch plate*
Pipe   *1½-inch DWV, 9 feet long cut into:*
           2 13-inch sections
           2 14-inch sections
           2 15-inch sections
           1 19½-inch section
Fittings *(to fit 1½-inch DWV pipe)*
           6 right-angle elbows

This unusual coffee table can be called modern or Art Deco, as you wish. Not only is it beautiful in its own way, it is also highly functional. It is easily cleaned, and easily folded for storage.

7. Folding Coffee Table

THE COFFEE TABLE illustrated consists of a 30-inch disc of ¼-inch-thick plate glass on a folding plastic frame support. The top of the glass is 17½ inches above the floor. With the glass removed, the open frame occupies a space 19 by 19 inches overall and 17¼ inches high. Folded, the required space is reduced to 4½ by 17 by 24 inches. Taken apart, of course, it's just a number of short pieces of pipe and right-angle fittings.

Construction is very simple. All that's required is to cut the pipe into the required lengths and assemble the frame. To permit complete take-apart, none of the joints are "locked." To permit simple folding, all the joints except two may be permanently locked with either cement or screws.

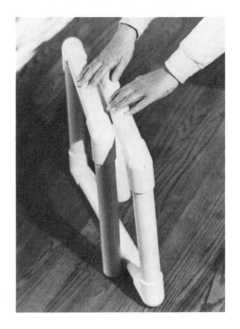

With the glass removed, the legs and frame fold neatly together. If you wish, you can construct the frame so that it may be completely disassembled into its component parts.

VARIATIONS   There are any number of ways this basic design can be varied or altered. Some are probably obvious, some may not be. No doubt readers can think of a few changes themselves.

Size   The disc diameter selected for this frame is arbitrary. It can be a few inches larger or smaller in diameter without disturbing the table's proportions or symmetry. The height of the frame also can be altered an inch or two up or down without problem. When this is done, of course, all the vertical pieces are made longer or shorter, as one wishes. But if the tabletop is brought up much higher, one must be certain to lock all the joints excepting the two necessary for folding the table. At the same time the overall dimensions of the frame must not be altered to make it smaller—which might be done if one were thinking about turning it into a flower stand or night table—unless the top is reduced also. A night table is shown in chapter 15.

The 1½-inch pipe size selected is about right for the size of the table. It might be reduced ¼ inch without much visual change. But this design will not look solid and stable with pipe under 1¼ inch. On the up side, 1¾-inch pipe is about as large a pipe diameter that can be used without the table looking bulky. Of course, the strength of the pipe is no consideration. Even 3/3-inch pipe would be strong enough.

Proportions   The frame in its open position presents a square when one looks down. This shape is not critical, and can be altered if one wishes. But we believe that a square within a circle is more attractive than a rectangle within a circle.

Now, should one have an oval or rectangular piece of plate glass for the table top, a rectangular frame can be made easily. The two short horizontal pieces can remain as they are or be shortened. The long, single horizontal piece of pipe is made longer. By making the frame longer than it is wide, it will support a rectangular or oval plate that much more securely.

Glass was selected for this table top because we believe the frame is unusual and attractive. But should marble or wood be desired, there is no reason not to use either. However, in the case of wood, which is comparatively light, it is suggested that one drill up through the horizontal pipes and drive wood screws partway into the bottom of the table top. Also, if most of the frame is to be hidden, smaller pipe can be used.

Different material

The pipe is cut to the necessary lengths. The pipe ends are fitted into the right-angle fittings. The assembly is placed on a perfectly flat and level surface. With a square of some kind, all the legs are checked to be sure they are perfectly vertical. With the aid of a ruler, the frame is made to form a perfect square. The glass is placed gently atop the frame. The distance from the edge of the frame to the floor is measured at several points. If the tabletop is not perfectly level, the overly high legs are shortened. When this is done, the high leg should be reduced by no more than a little at a time. It is all too easy to go overboard doing this and end up with all the legs woefully short.

PROCEDURE

When the frame is perfectly square and all the legs are alike and the table top is level, and all the legs are vertical, each leg and its associate pipe end is marked with a pencil. In addition, each leg

Locking the joints

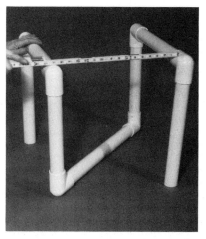

(Left) Here the frame parts have been assembled and the frame extended into its normal shape.

(Right) If you plan to lock any or all of the parts together, check the extended frame to make certain leg heights are correct and that the joints are all correct.

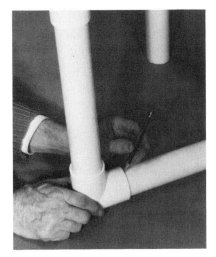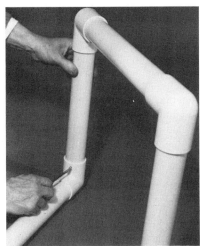

(Left) If you plan to cement a joint, mark the pipe-to-fitting relationship, as suggested in Chapter 4.

(Right) As an alternative to cementing the joints you can lock them with screws. This technique is also discussed in Chapter 4.

end and pipe end is numbered. A china pencil (grease pencil) is best for this. With the marks in place one can be certain that when the frame is disassembled and reassembled it will be perfectly square. Now, if the joints are to be cemented, this should be done as suggested in chapter 4. If the legs are to be screw-joined to fittings, clearance holes should be drilled through the fittings. The frame is reassembled and a pilot hole drilled through the pipe ends. Next, the screw holes are countersunk—if flat head screws are being used—and the screws are installed.

PARTS LIST/DRAIN PIPE COFFEE TABLE

Glass	30-inch diameter, ¼-inch plate glass
Pipe	3½-inch DWV, 6 feet long, divided into:
	4 17-inch sections
	3/4-inch PVC, 15 feet long, divided into:
	4 24-inch sections
	4 18-inch sections
Fittings	(To fit 3/4-inch pipe)
	8 caps
Screws	8 2-inch #10 sheet-metal screws

8. Drainpipe Coffee Table

THE COFFEE TABLE illustrated here was designed and constructed for use as a coffee table, obviously, and to illustrate the wide range of plastic pipe available and how this range might be utilized for furniture. The word "drainpipe" was selected because the vertical portions of the table, its legs, are made of sections of 3½-inch O.D. DWV or drainpipe. The particular pipe selected is gray. The horizontal bars are cream colored.

Like the preceding design, this table is also made to be topped by a 30-inch disc of ¼-inch or thicker glass plate. The weight of the glass is sufficient to hold it in place. Since the legs are 17 inches high, the overall height of the table is, of course, 17 inches plus the thickness of the glass.

This coffee table is a little more difficult to construct than the

67

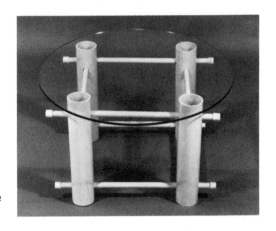

The coffee table by itself. Here you can see more clearly how the cross bars are positioned.

preceding table, the difference being the need to cut fairly accurately positioned holes in the table legs. Other than this, construction is very simple.

VARIATIONS   The size and diameters of the legs and crossbars can vary. The crossbars can be fastened to the outside of the legs, or they can be crossed. Leg spacing and leg arrangement can vary, even going to three legs if desired, although this makes hole placement difficult. One thing that cannot be done, however, is replacement of the glass top with a wood or marble top. In the case of wood, its weight would be insufficient, unless it was thick oak or a similar heavy wood. Marble would, of course, be heavy enough, but would hide much of the frame, making the table look entirely different.

Size   If desired, the size of the glass plate could be reduced to as little as possibly 20 inches, in which case the legs would probably be brought closer together—but no less than 14 inches overall. The present 30-inch disc could remain and the leg spacing be reduced from its present 21 to 19 inches overall (not counting the projecting crossbars). On the other hand, if a 35-inch piece of glass is desired, it must be at least ⅜ inch thick, and it would be advisable to increase the diameter of the legs from their present 3½-inch size to a 4- or 4½-inch O.D. The crossbars too should be upped from their present size to 1 inch I.D.

Outdoor application   The same basic design could be used to make an outdoor table. Leg height would have to be increased to 29 inches, tabletop diameter to 35 or more inches to make it useful for three or four people. Leg pipe and crossbar pipe size would have to be increased as suggested. Outdoors leg spacing should also be increased, say to a minimum of 29 by 29 inches. The reason is the prevention of tipping. As a further obstacle to tipping, the legs might be filled with concrete. This is done by plugging the bottoms of the legs with wet paper, after which some cement is poured into the legs, followed by small stones and more cement. Although this will increase the weight of the table considerably, it still will not be too heavy to move if need be.

Now the tabletop has to be secured. If a glass disc is being used, it is best to go to ½-inch glass, which, unfortunately is very expensive. A good alternative is either marble or slate, both of which are sufficiently heavy to remain in place even in a very strong wind.

Should even greater security be desired, the legs should not be filled with concrete. Instead, the top three inches are left open. Then four discs of 1-inch plywood are cut. (The diameter of each disc should be slightly less than the inside diameter of the legs.) With epoxy cement, the wood discs are fastened to the underside of the tabletop. Each disc is carefully positioned in vertical alignment with each table leg. When the tabletop is placed on its legs, each disc rests within the top of each leg. Now, clearance holes are driven through the tops of each leg—say two holes per leg. Next, screws are driven through the clearance holes and into the wood. In this way the tabletop can be fastened permanently to its legs.

The first step is to make the legs. Three-and-a-half-inch-O.D. PVC **PROCEDURE** drainpipe is cut into four legs, each exactly 17 inches long, assuming a coffee table is being made. It is important to make the cuts perfectly square across the pipe. If a miter box large enough to accommodate the drain pipe is not available, the technique for cutting large-diameter pipe suggested in chapter 3 should be followed. If a perfectly square or even cut is not made, this should be disregarded until the coffee table has been assembled. Then the high spots can be filed down if necessary.

A straight-edged piece of paper is wrapped
around the large diameter pipe as a cutting guide.

Drilling
holes in
the legs

There are four crossbars that go completely through the legs; thus sixteen holes are needed for these bars. Four bars enter the legs but do not pass through. Thus eight more holes for these bars are needed. The illustrations will show how the bars and their holes are arranged.

The centers of the holes for the "through" bars are positioned 2½ inches down from the tops of the legs, and 3 inches up from the bottoms of the legs. Vertically, the holes are in perfect alignment, meaning that they are directly above one another. Laterally, the holes are also in alignment—each hole is duplicated by an identical hole on the other side of the leg.

To start, a straight line is drawn in pencil down the side of the pipe. The pipe is measured 2½ inches down from the top, and this spot is marked on the vertical line. Three inches are measured up on the same line and another mark is made. Next, the top of the line is extended onto the edge of the pipe. The same is done with the lower end of the line. The pipe is now stood on end, and the top of the line carried directly across the diameter of the pipe, being marked with a pencil. Then, the edge of the combination square is placed atop the two marks so that you can look directly down. If the mark has been carried accurately across the top of the pipe, the square will have visually divided the pipe into two equal halves. If not, the second mark is moved. This done, the process is repeated at the other end of the pipe. Then the two marks are connected with a pencil line. The line is measured up and down, and the centers of the holes to be drilled are marked.

At this point there are four marks locating the centers of four holes that have to be drilled. The holes are to be in pairs, each member of a pair to be in line with the other.

With a small twist drill, holes are now made in the pipe at each of the hole marks. Following this, a ⅞-inch Speedbor bit is used in the drill motor to enlarge each hole. This bit size is needed be-

Using the combinations square as an aid to locating the center of the hole to be drilled for the horizontal pipe. In this case the square has been extended exactly 2½ inches and the distance is marked off on the pre-drawn vertical line.

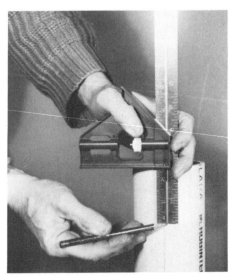

cause this is the O.D. of the pipe used for all the bars. Drilling is from the outside of the pipe inwards. The drill motor is held just as steadily as possible, and only a very light pressure is applied to the bit. There will be considerable vibration as the bit goes through the last of the plastic. The bit will also leave a little edge within the hole. This can be filed down.

This entire operation is repeated on the remaining three legs. Next, the through bars—these are the 24-inch-long pieces of ¾-inch I.D. pipe—are slid through the holes as illustrated. If the holes have been drilled accurately there will be no difficulty doing this. If the holes are a little off, the bars may have to be forced through. Should the holes be so far out of line that the bars cannot be pushed through the holes, it is a good idea to try shifting the legs around. Sometimes an error in one pair of holes is offset or corrected by an error in an opposing pair of holes. If this doesn't work, the bars might be bent a little, or one side of the holes enlarged with a file where necessary.

The next step consists of drilling two more holes in each leg. These holes are for the short bars, the bars that do not pass through the leg. The holes are positioned vertically, one above the other, on a line at right angles to the crossbar holes. The upper of the short-bar holes is below the upper through-bar. The lower of the pair of holes is above the lower through-bar. When the holes have been drilled and the short bars positioned, the clearance between the short and the through bars should be minimal—one-fourth of an inch or less. The reason for this is that the two bars are going to be fastened together at their crossover point with a screw, thus locking the entire assembly together.

With the through bars in position—projecting one to two inches beyond the legs, as desired—the legs are stood on their ends and positioned to form a perfect square or rectangle. The illustrations will show where the short bars go. To locate their

The through bars have been positioned and the legs have been stood up on end. The folding rule is used to temporarily space the legs the desired distance apart. In this case, 18 inches from the inside of one pipe to the other.

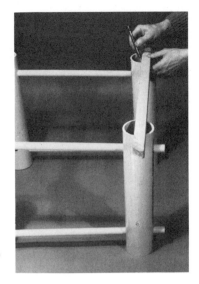

A straight-edged stick is used to carry a straight line across the centers of the two pipe legs.

holes, it is necessary to draw an imaginary line across the tops of all the legs. This is done by placing a long straight-edged stick across the top of a pair of legs and marking the center of each top. Next, this mark is extended down the side of the pipe in a long, perfectly vertical line. (This is exactly what was done before to locate the other holes.) On this line the center of the upper short-bar hole will be three-and-a-half inches down (one inch below the center of the through bar). The lower short-bar hole will be four inches up from the bottom of the leg on the same line.

Assembly With the holes all drilled, the legs are simply placed upright on a flat surface and the bars inserted. The short bars must go all the way into the legs, meaning that the short-bar ends touch the inside surface of the pipe. Now the legs are adjusted until the through bars project an equal distance beyond the pipe legs. In the coffee table illustrated, the bars project one inch beyond the pipe before the caps are positioned.

Now a check is made to be certain that all the legs are perfectly

(Left) Holes have been drilled and the short bars have been positioned. Now the combination square is used to make certain each leg is perfectly vertical.

(Right) The distance each cross bar extends beyond its leg is carefully measured. Corrections are made if necessary. Following this the legs are checked for verticality again.

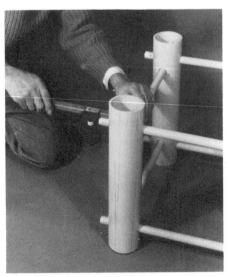

Next the diagonal distances between facing legs is measured. When the two diagonals are equal, the legs form a perfect square. If not, adjust as necessary.

vertical, that they are spaced the proper distances apart. If necessary, some of the short bars can be shortened or replaced, but their ends must fit tightly against the inside of the pipe legs. A further check must be made to see that the legs form a perfect rectangle or square. This can be done with a square or by measuring the diagonals—the distances from one leg diagonally across the space to the other leg. When the diagonals are equal the corners are square.

Next, the bar ends must be drilled through and locked together with screws. This is easily done. The only problem is not to move any of the table parts while doing so. A small-diameter twist drill should be used. The drill and motor are positioned vertically above the center of each leg, and drilling goes down through the crossed pair of bar ends. This is followed with the correct-size pilot drill and clearance drill. A two-inch #10 sheet-metal screw is used to join the bars together. When the first pair of bars has been fastened together, the assembly is rechecked to make certain nothing has changed. Now a second pair of bar ends is drilled

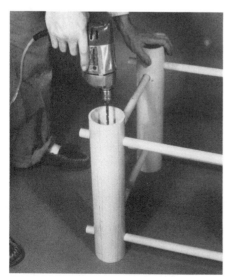

When everything is square and ship-shape, carefully drill a 5/32-inch pilot hole through both pipes, then a 3/16-inch clearance holes through the top pipe only. Then join the two pipes with a 2-inch, #10 sheet metal screw. The glass merely sits on top. The caps are held in place on the pipe ends by friction alone. There is no need to cement them.

and joined. Again, a check is made to see that nothing has shifted out of position before work is resumed. This process continues— one pair of bar ends at a time until they are all fastened together.

Completion   Joining the bar ends together might pull the legs out of position a little. If the change cannot be easily seen or if one leg has lifted a fraction of an inch, nothing need be done. The weight of the glass will bring it down. If the screws have pulled the assembly badly out of alignment, the trouble is due to inaccurately drilled holes. Cold-bending one of the bars is one possible solution to the problem. Another is turning a bar around and possibly redrilling alongside the old hole. Generally, a little fudging here and there will bring everything beautifully into line.

Now all that remains is to remove the company's printing with a little paint remover and wash the fingerprints off. The final step is simply placing the glass on top.

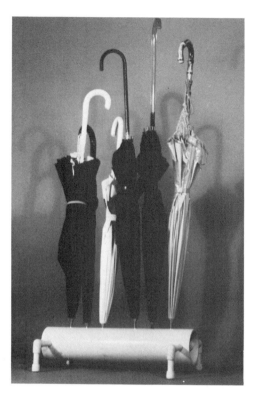

PARTS LIST/"DACHSHUND" UMBRELLA STAND

Pipe	3½-inch O.D., DWV,
	1 section, 18 inches long
	1½-inch I.D., DWV,
	1 section, 14 inches long
	⅝ inch O.D. PVC, 2½ feet long cut into:
	2 11-inch sections
	4 2-inch sections
Fittings	To accept ⅝-inch O.D. pipe:
	4 90-degree elbows
	4 caps
Screws	2 1-inch #8 flathead sheet-metal screws

9. Umbrella Stand

WITH ITS FAT, low-slung body and short, bent legs this umbrella stand looks somewhat like a dachshund, but unlike the little dog, this stand doesn't have to be walked.

As designed, the stand is made to hold seven umbrellas in an upright position. Unlike other stands, this one doesn't require much space and can be placed alongside a wall in an entranceway. It stands five inches high, is seventeen inches long, and has a foot spread of a little under thirteen inches. In operation, the metal tip of an umbrella is slipped into the holes in the outer pipe and the inner pipe. In this way the umbrella is held in a vertical position.

DESIGN VARIATIONS A craftsperson with the skill and time can carve a head and rump for the little beast. The larger pipe could be extended and its ends closed with caps. If this is done a few drain holes should be drilled in the bottom of the pipe, so that moisture can leave the pipe.

A larger-diameter pipe can be used for the body. (This one has an O.D. of 3½ inches.) And of course the other dimensions can be varied somewhat. If this is done, however, the diameter of the outer pipe should not be reduced below 2½ inches O.D., or the stand will be tippy. By the same token, the spread of the legs should not be reduced to much under 9 inches.

In the design illustrated, the legs go through the body of the creature. This can be varied, if desired, by using one-inch or larger-diameter pipe for the legs, and then, instead of running the legs through the body, fastening the legs to one side of the body pipe. This can be done by cutting a shallow curve in the side of the leg pipe and then fastening it to the side of the large-diameter pipe with a pair of screws.

A stand of the same size and design could be made to support more umbrellas. At present, all the umbrellas stand in a vertical position and there is a 2-inch space between holes. If the spacing betwen support holes were reduced from 2 inches to 1½ inches, it would be possible to support 10 umbrellas within the 15½ inches between the small-diameter cross pipes that form the legs. However, since 1½ inches of space between umbrellas would make it difficult to place and remove umbrellas that adjoined one another, it would be necessary to secure more space by angling umbrellas alternately away from the perpendicular. In other words, one umbrella would pitch toward us at an angle of 15 degrees from vertical, while the following would pitch an equal amount in the other direction.

There is nothing wrong with this design, except that the fully occupied stand would take a little more space, and it would be much more difficult to align the alternately pitched holes in the two pipe lengths.

CONSTRUCTION

Making the body The stand body is an 18-inch-long section of 3½-inch O.D. pipe, with both ends cut squarely across. The first step in making the body consists of drawing a straight line down the length of the pipe. By straight we mean that the entire length of the line drawn must be centered over the pipe's diameter. On this line, 3 inches are measured in from either end of the pipe and a mark made. Then another series of marks is made on the line, each mark ex-

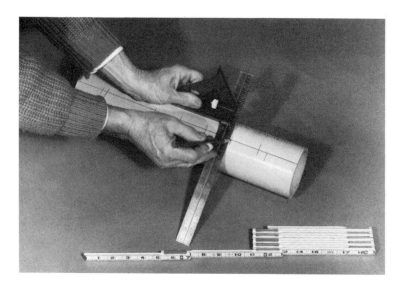

A line is drawn the length of the large pipe, then, starting 3 inches from the end of the pipe, a mark is made on the line every 2 inches.

actly 2 inches from the other. If all measuring and calculations are correct, the last mark will be 3 inches from the end of the pipe. Now a ⅜-inch hole is drilled through each mark—7 holes in all. Countersink each hole an equal distance.

Next, a 14-inch-long piece of 1½-inch I.D. pipe is secured. Again, a straight line is drawn down its side. On this line 1 inch is measured in from either end. A mark is made at each of these points on the line. Starting with this mark, a series of marks is made, leaving exactly 2 inches between marks. This done, a ⅜-inch hole is drilled through each mark for a total of 7 holes. Each hole is countersunk. This pipe is put aside for the moment.

The large-diameter pipe—the body of the "dachshund"—is now stood on its "tail." Starting with the line drawn for the holes, a line is drawn across the pipe and down its side. This line should be directly opposite the first line. In other words, if the pipe were

A pilot hole is drilled through each mark on the line.

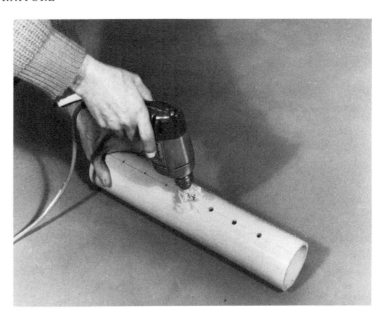

Each hole is enlarged with a ⅜-inch bit and countersunk.

cut lengthwise along the two parallel lines, it would be cut exactly in half.

On the second line, 4 inches are measured from the pipe end, and the spot is marked. Now an 11/64-inch clearance hole is drilled through the mark. At the other end of the same line another 4 inches in from the pipe end are measured off, and a second clearance hole is drilled here. Both holes are countersunk.

The small-diameter pipe is now placed within the large-diameter pipe. Both are placed on the workbench. With a number of pencils, the two sets of drilled holes are aligned. Now the assembly is upended. With another pencil, the last pair of holes made is poked through and their location marked on the smaller, inner

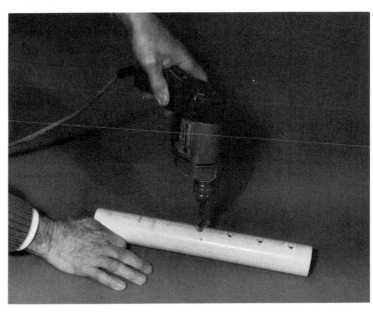

Starting 1 inch from the end of the smaller diameter pipe, seven holes are drilled, each 2 inches apart.

The smaller pipe is placed within the larger pipe. The drilled holes are aligned with the aid of pencils.

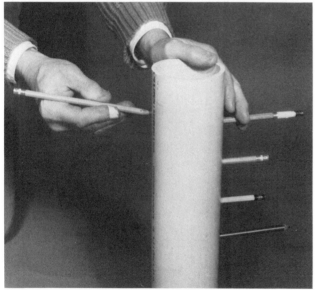

The position of the inner pipe in relation to the outer pipe is located by means of pencil marks made through a pair of previously drilled holes in the larger pipe. Note the pencils are still in place.

pipe. The pipes and pencils are disassembled. Next, pilot holes are drilled through the two marks just made. A ⅛-inch bit is used. Next, the small pipe within the larger pipe is replaced. The holes just drilled are aligned and the pipes fastened together with 1-inch #8 flathead sheet-metal screws.

To check on the work thus far, the assembly—the joined pipes—is laid back on the bench. Pencils are slid through the holes in the outer and larger pipe—the body of the stand—into the holes in the inner pipe. Hopefully, all the holes line up.

Constructing
the legs
The legs are fastened to pipes that pass through the body of the stand. These pipes must be perfectly horizontal in relation to the pairs of holes, which are in vertical alignment. So, with the pencils still in place, and perfectly vertical, a horizontal line is drawn across one end of the larger pipe. (This simply means marking the edge of the pipe.) These lines or marks are carried down the sides of the pipe for an inch or two. Following, on these two lines, a measurement is made, just one inch in from the end of the pipe, and the spot is marked. The exact same is done at the other end of the stand body. With a ⅛-inch drill, pilot holes are drilled through these four marks. Then, since ⅝-inch O.D. bars will be used to carry the legs, ⅝-inch holes are drilled into the stand body, centered on the pilot holes.

Each leg bar is 11 inches long. This can be varied an inch or two either way if desired. Each bar is cemented in place with the help of a ⅝-inch I.D. slip-fitting cut in half. The pieces of the fitting are spread apart and cemented onto the leg bar. When the cement hardens, the bar cannot move in either direction, nor turn.

The first step is to cut the two fittings in half. Then one end of each piece of fitting is rounded to make it conform, more or less,

Holes are drilled through the sides of the outer pipe. The ⅝-inch Speedbor bit is used only after a pilot hole has been drilled. A very light touch is necessary to produce a smooth hole.

A leg bar is tried in the holes. This bar or pipe must be horizontal when the umbrella holes—where the pencils have been temporarily positioned—are vertical.

Tail-end view of the stand. A leg bar has been slipped through the stand body and two halves of a slip fitting. Now cement is applied to the leg bar. The halves of the slip fitting will then be separated and pushed against the inside of the body pipe.

to the inner curve of the body pipe. One end of one leg bar is slipped into one side of the stand body. The two pieces of fitting are slid onto the pipe. The leg bar or pipe is slid the rest of the way through the stand body. The leg bar is centered, and also pencil-marked so that it can be centered quickly again. This done, the cut fittings are turned and adjusted so that they are snug against the inside of the pipe. Fitting position is marked in relation to the leg bar. Now the two fittings are pushed toward each other. A generous dollop of cement is spread on the leg pipe alongside the insides of the large pipe or stand body. Now the pieces of slip fitting are quickly pushed back into place; it's important to make certain that they are snug and tight and that the

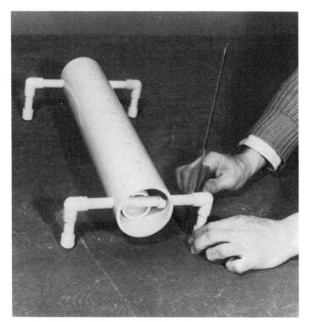

Each short piece of ½-inch pipe has been cemented to a cap and to a right angle. Cement is placed on the end of a leg bar and the angle is positioned on the end of the bar. As soon as this is done the combination square is used to make certain the angle is perfectly vertical.

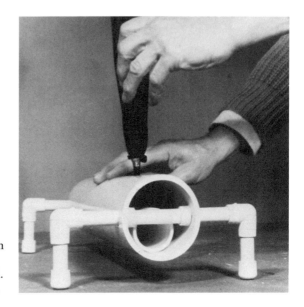

If all has gone well with the project, the tip of an umbrella will reach through the outer pipe and into the inner pipe while the umbrella is vertical. Note the position of the halves of the slip fitting.

leg bar or pipe is centered. When the cement hardens the leg bar will be locked firmly in place.

The four legs themselves consist of four right-angle bends. two-inch stumpy legs, and four caps to go over the ends of the legs. All the fittings are sized to take ⅝-inch O.D. pipe and are fastened with cement.

Side view of empty cart.

PARTS LIST/TEA CART

Pipe	1¼-inch DWV 22 feet long, cut into:
	4 22-inch; 4 12-inch; 4 24-inch; 1 13-inch; 2 3½-inch sections
	½-inch PVC, 14 feet long, cut into: 4 25½-inch sections 4 15-inch sections
Fittings	(To fit 1¼-inch DWV pipe) 10 90-degree angles 2 45-degree angles 2 caps
Glass	Double-weight window glass or ¼-inch plate 2 pieces, 14½ by 24 inches, corners removed
Screws	4 2½-inch #12 flathead sheet-metal screws 4 ¾-inch #8 flathead sheet-metal screws
Wood	2 × 4, 14 inches long, cut into 4 4-inch pieces
Hardware	4 1⅝-inch diameter plastic-wheel stem casters

10. Tea Cart

THE TEA CART pictured is made of 1¼-inch DWV pipe. It stands 31 inches high, is 17 inches wide, and 30 inches long; and rides on 1⅝-inch plastic stem casters. Each tray or level is made of double-weight window glass (¼-inch plate would be better), 14½ by 24 inches in size with the corners cut off. The top tray is 23 inches above the floor, the lower tray 8 inches. As only the caster supports and screws are of metal, there is little in the way of weather that can harm this tea cart.

There is not too much that comes to mind in design variations. VARIATIONS Obviously, pipe diameter could be changed. However, this designer believes that the use of 1-inch pipe would reduce the cart's charm, though its strength would not be seriously impaired. To go

Corner view.

in the other direction would, again to this designer, be a mistake. To use 1½-inch DWV pipe on a wagon of this size would make it much too "blocky."

Size The overall size of the cart could be increased a few inches in width and length. Its present height is about usual for a wagon or cart this size. If, however, a cart is wanted for actual utilitarian purposes, its trays could be made a few inches higher—but not more than an inch or two, or the cart would look like it belonged in a restaurant.

Trays The glass could be replaced with wood panels. These would look best if carried in slots cut into the tray frame pipe. A light wood panel might go well with the plastic pipe. However, if the cart is to carry flowerpots—and many are used for this purpose—the wood trays would be a problem as water would eventually stain the wood no matter how careful one might be.

The tray guardrails are merely single lengths of pipe. This is certainly not the best of all possible guardrail designs, but there is no simple alternative. If larger-diameter guard rail pipes were installed and vertical pipes were run in a fencelike arrangement all around the tray, this would mean not only a lot of work but a lot of grief. Whenever two pieces of pipe or whatever are placed close to one another, it becomes easy for the eye to spot errors. One cannot tell whether two long poles two feet apart are perfectly parallel or not. But bring them to within, let us say, a quarter of an inch of each other, and a misalignment of one-eighth inch or even less will be spotted quickly. The alternative to a picket fence of pipe around the tray that is practical would be a narrow, perforated plastic strip, just as high as one wants the guard rail to be. Unfortunately, this type of pierced strip is not manufactured. It is made in metal, but not in the widths needed, and not of a suitable metal.

In the present design the vertical pipes that form the corners are fitted into arcs cut in the corners of the frames forming the trays. This is a lot easier to do than it may appear. One alternative would be to introduce a number of T's into the tray frames. This would save corner cutting but would increase the cost of the project by the cost of the necessary T's. It would also bring the legs of the cart closer together, which would reduce its stability. Cross fittings could also be used. The problems here would again be the reduced spacing between the cart legs and wheels, and the difficulty of securing the crosses. Few suppliers stock them.

Corner poles

The best alternative to the present corner pole or pipe design would be the use of "side-feed right-angle" fittings. These fittings would join three pipe ends to form a corner. Unfortunately, this fitting is not manufactured for plumbing. If it is seen on commercial plastic pipe furniture, it has been made specially for that furniture manufacturer.

The start is made by cutting all the pipe into the required pieces, as listed in the parts list at the beginning of this chapter. All the burrs on the ends of the pipe are removed with sandpaper. A little pipe will be left over.

PROCEDURE

As seen in the illustration, there are two pipe frames that support the sheets of glass. Each frame has four right-angle—90-degree-angle—fittings that form their corners. An arc has been cut into each corner, and into this arc the corner post nests or fits, held in place by a single large screw driven through the corner. The arcs are to be cut in eight right angles.

Cutting the corners

A scrap of 1¼-inch pipe is clamped firmly in the vise. The pipe is used to support a corner angle. Now a curved section is cut out of the corner with a coping saw. The contour of the curve should be identical to the exterior of the 1¼-inch pipes that serve as corner posts. The depth of the curve should be approximately equal to ⅓ the diameter of the corner-post pipe. The saw will, of course, cut through two thicknesses of pipe. In other words, two cuts will be made simultaneously. This means that the saw blade must be held at right angles to the scrap of pipe being used to hold the cor-

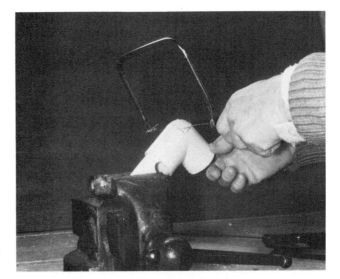

To cut an arc out of the corner of a 90-degree fitting, draw two lines indicating the area in which you wish to make your cut. Then saw away with a coping saw.

Drill a pilot hole directly into the joint angle of the fitting.

ner fitting. Now, with the corner arc cut and removed, a section of 1¼-inch pipe is tried in the cut. If it doesn't fit correctly—and this will be obvious—sandpaper is wrapped around the pipe and the cut sandpapered until it is the proper depth and shape. This operation must be performed on a total of eight corner fittings, and all the cut depths should be reasonably alike.

All this accomplished, the corner fittings are replaced on the piece of scrap pipe and a pilot hole is drilled directly into the joint angle—in other words, through the fitting in direct line with the cut that has been made. This hole is where a screw will be positioned, to enter and hold the corner post in place.

With scraps of lumber, construct a large right angle. Assemble the legs within the angle and then draw two lines across the legs indicating the centers of the two frames.

Preparing the legs

Several pieces of scrap lumber are fastened to the work table or board, so as to form a large right angle. The legs are assembled side by side within this right angle. All the legs are now parallel to and in line with each other. From the leg end that will be the bottom, 5 inches are measured up, and then an additional 15 inches. These two points are marked, and with the aid of a combination square are carried across all four legs. These marks indicate the center of each frame. In other words, when screws are driven through the pilot holes that have just been drilled in the corner fittings, the screws will be on these lines.

Installing the casters

On hand are four pieces of 2 × 4, each more or less four inches long. One piece is stood on end, and with a kitchen knife or broad chisel, split vertically along its grain to form a rough dowel approximately 1¼ inches in diameter. Some cardboard is wrapped

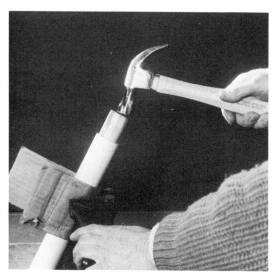

Drive the dowel you have cut from the piece of 2x4 into the end of the leg.

Drill an 11/64-inch hole through the side of the pipe, but not into the wood. Countersink the hole and then drive a ¾-inch, flat head screw into the wood.

Drill a pilot hole down the center of the dowel and follow with a ⅜-inch bit.

around one cart leg—this will be one of the 24-inch pieces of pipe just marked—and the leg is placed, bottom end up, in the vise. Now the dowel that has just been made is driven into the end of the pipe. When the dowel is flush with the pipe end, an 11/64-inch hole is drilled and countersunk through the pipe—with care being taken not to drill into the wood. This accomplished, the

Drive the caster support all the way into the hole.

dowel is locked in place by driving a ¾-inch, #8 flathead screw through the hole and into the wood.

The next step is to drill a ⅛-inch pilot hole down the length of the dowel, taking care to center the hole and keep the drill parallel to the length of the pipe. This is followed with a ⅜-inch drill bit, assuming that this is the hole size suited to the casters selected. After this, the caster support is driven into the hole. Now the caster can be snapped into place when desired.

At this point there is still that large right angle on the work board. If not, one should be made from scrap lumber. One frame is assembled; the sides are made from the 12- and 22-inch pieces. It is placed on the work board within the right-angle jig or guide. Now

Assembling the frames

Assemble one frame. Lay it flat within the scrap-wood right angle frame as shown and measure its width and length to make certain all parts are correctly sized.

it should be checked to make certain that it is truly rectangular. If one pipe has been cut a little short, it can be cemented to the corner fitting, leaving a little clearance inside. Or all the other pipes can be shortened accordingly. In any case, only the short pipe is to be cemented. All the other joints are assembled dry. With one frame checked out, the operation is repeated with the second frame.

Assembling the cart   The frame is removed from the jig or guide. A leg is placed in the jig, pressed up against one side of the jig. One frame is positioned atop the leg. The frame is positioned vertically and centered over one of the lines drawn across the leg. (This would be either the line on the 5-inch or 15-inch mark.) Now a pilot hole is drilled through the predrilled hole in the fitting and into the leg. The frame is removed and a 7/32-inch clearance hole drilled in the fitting alone. After reassembly, a 2½-inch #12 screw is driven through the fitting and into the leg.

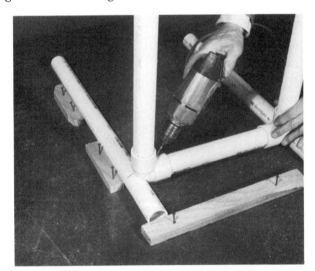

Hold one frame in position over a leg. Drill through the corner fitting (following the pre-drilled pilot hole) into the leg. Then drill a 7/32-inch clearance hole through the fitting alone. Then fasten the fitting to the leg with a 2½-inch #12 screw.

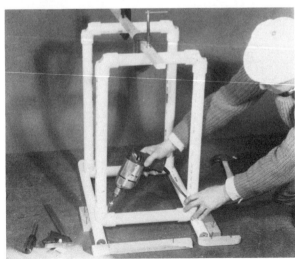

Use clamps and a length of wood to hold both frames in proper alignment. Drill the balance of the fittings and fasten all the corner fittings to the legs with screws. Note the scraps of lumber holding the second leg in proper position on the work board.

A second leg is positioned beneath the screwed-in place frame. Scrap lumber is positioned and nailed alongside the second leg, with care taken to keep the second leg in line and parallel with the first. The second frame is positioned over the second mark on the first leg. The second frame is drilled and screw-fastened to this leg. Next, with a board and clamps, both frames are locked in a vertical position—after it has been ascertained that the frames are parallel and centered over the proper marks on the legs. Now holes can be drilled for the remaining screws, which are then installed.

The cart frame is now completely assembled. It is stood upright on its legs. The centers of the holes that have to be drilled for the guardrail pipes are located and marked. The upper rails are centered 2 inches down from the top of the corner. The lower rail is centered 9¼ inches up from the bottom of the corner post. These dimensions are laid out with the square—it is easier and more ac-

Installing the guardrails

Using the combination square to measure down from the upper end of each leg to locate a guard rail hole.

Drilling one of the holes for a guard rail.

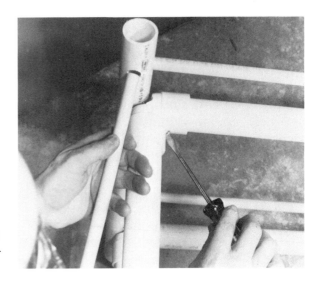

Loosen the corner screw to slip the ends of the guard rails into the holes in the legs. Note that the cart handle has been removed.

curate this way. Pilot holes should be made first, and followed with the ⅝-inch Speedbor bit.

To install the guard rails, one corner screw is loosened—but not removed—at a time. This will permit moving the corner post away from the frame and sliding the ends of the guard rails into their respective holes. The cart handle is just pushed into place.

DISASSEMBLY All the parts of the tea cart can be permanently locked together with a little cement at each joint. However, this is not necessary. The eight corner screws will hold everything tightly together. To disassemble, then, all that is needed is to remove these screws.

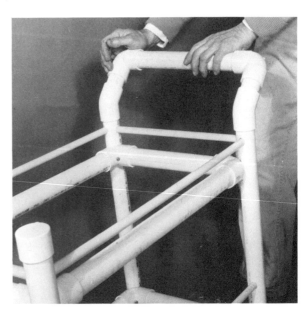

The cart handle is replaced by just pushing it on.

PARTS LIST/FLOWER STAND NIGHT TABLE

Top	*2-inch thick, 15-inch-diameter wood block*
Pipe	*1½-inch DWV, 6 feet long, cut into:*
	1 22-inch section
	1 14-inch section
	1 11-inch section
	1 6½-inch section
	1 5-inch section
Fittings	*(To fit 1½-inch DWV pipe)*
	4 90-degree angles
	1 transition
	1 flange (galvanized iron)
	1 cap
Screws	*3 1-inch #8 flathead*

Sturdy, portable and dependable, the stand can serve attractively in many different ways.

11. Flower Stand/Night Table

THE FLOWER STAND or night table pictured may look like a new-era bar stool, but it is not. It has been designed to stand beside one's bed at night, dutifully supporting a table lamp—and possibly a snifter of brandy—or to hold a flowering plant somewhere in the living room.

As illustrated, the little table stands 27 inches high. Its top is 15 inches in diameter and its base is 18 by 15½ inches.

The top shown is a 2-inch-thick maple chopping block. It was selected because it is both attractive and ready to go. Except for the need to give it several spray coats of clear lacquer to keep the wood from being stained, there is nothing else to be done to it. A thinner disc of wood would serve as well, but to this artist, it

VARIATIONS

Using different tops

93

would not look as attractive. Perhaps it would "work" with 1-inch pipe and an overall height of, say, 20 inches.

A marble top could also be used. If 2-inch marble is available, the given dimensions obtain. If the marble's thickness is only about one inch, this designer suggests, as before, a thinner pipe and a lower top-height.

The wood top is fastened to the galvanized iron flange with wood screws. This is impractical with marble (though it can be done). To fasten the flange to marble, glass, plastic, or even wood (if desired), epoxy cement is used—not that miracle or magic glue, which will not work properly in this instance. Before applying the cement, the flange is prepared. It is placed flat side down on a sheet of coarse sandpaper, then moved to and fro until all the little rough spots on the bottom of the flange have been removed and a relatively smooth, flat surface has been produced. Next the flange is centered on the underside of the marble, its postion marked with a pencil. The flange is then removed. A generous coat of epoxy is applied to the underside of the marble, the flange is repositioned, and flange and marble are placed in the oven which is set to about 200 degrees. This will insure a strong bond.

Size changes   The illustrated stand utilizes 1½-inch DWV pipe. This can be reduced to 1¼ inches and still retain the same top and other dimensions. But going to 1-inch pipe requires going to a 1-inch-thick top and reducing the height of the stand. Not that it becomes tippy with thinner pipe; it just looks somewhat weak and spindly. On the other hand, I don't believe there is anything to be gained visually by going to thicker pipe.

One can, of course, follow the same design and increase the diameter of the top. If this is done, the overall dimensions of the base should be increased. At present the maximum base width is 18 inches for a top diameter of 15 inches. At a height of 27 inches, these proportions not only give the appearance of stability; they are stable. So, if one goes to a larger top, the span of the base is increased proportionately.

One-and-a-half-inch pipe will allow a top of about 20–22 inches without any visual problem. A larger top requires an increase in the pipe diameter. With a 30-inch-diameter top it would be wise to use—and again this is an estimate—2-inch pipe, with a 30-inch base. After assembly and cementing, I'd fill this base with cement just to provide stability. I would also not only cement all the joints—excepting the lower end of the center pipe—but would use a plastic primer on the joints before applying the usual cement. The primer is applied with a small soft brush, which is easy enough. But extreme care must be taken not to let the primer run over the pipe as it will permanently stain it. However, the combination of primer and cement produces a really welded joint; the two pieces of plastic become one forever, and then some.

All the pieces of pipe are cut to size as listed in the parts list at the beginning of the chapter.

The flange is centered on the bottom of the wood block and fastened to the wood with wood screws.

The transition fitting is screwed into the flange. The transition has screw threads at one end and will accept a pipe end at its other end. In this case the fitting is designed to accept 1½-inch DWV pipe. The pipe end should be tried in the fitting to see if all is well.

The base is assembled on a perfectly flat surface. Each joint is cemented and joined one joint at a time, with care taken to be sure that the joint is properly aligned before the cement sets. The elbow that points upwards and holds the leg in place should not be cemented at this time.

When the base has been assembled and cemented and the joints are hard, the upward-pointing elbow is positioned and the leg is installed in place—all dry. A straight stick is fastened to the side of the leg with some masking tape. Now, with the aid of the combination square, the leg is adjusted until it is perfectly verti-

PROCEDURE

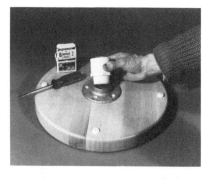

(Left) The flange has been fastened to the center of the underside of the top. Now the transition fitting is about to be screwed into place.

(Right) The top end of the pipe that serves as the single table leg is temporarily positioned within the fitting.

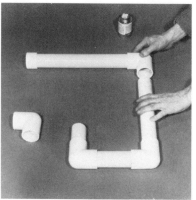

(Left) The base of the stand is assembled one joint at a time. Each joint is cemented fast. The elbow, or the 90-degree bend that is to face upwards is not cemented at this time.

(Right) With the aid of taped-in-place stick and a square, the last elbow is cemented to the base. The leg need not be cemented to the upward facing elbow.

cal. Pencil marks are made on the elbow and the lower pipe. Now the elbow can be removed and cement applied to the lower pipe. Then the leg is reassembled, again with the square to position it vertically.

DISASSEMBLY   As the little table stands now the leg is not cemented to the transition fitting beneath the wood top, nor to the upended elbow. For ordinary use the 1½-inch pipe resting a little more than 1 inch in the lower and upper fitting is perfectly snug and secure. There is no need either to cement or screw-fasten these joints. They can be left dry and the table disassembled at these two points.

However, if the pipe diameter is reduced, screws should at least be used to join the vertical leg to its two fittings. With a much larger tabletop, the table might be tried for stability before deciding to give up portability and to use screws or cement on the two joints.

Elegant in its simplicity, this dining room table is just the right size for two or four.

PARTS LIST/DINING ROOM TABLE

Glass	36 by 36 inches, ⅝-inch thick
Pipe	1½-inch DWV, 22 feet long cut into:
	4 4½-inch sections
	4 4¼-inch sections
	9 24-inch sections
Fittings	(for 1½-inch DWV pipe)
	6 T's
	8 90-degree elbows

12. Dining Room Table

THE DINING ROOM TABLE illustrated and described here is not only elegant and ultra-formal; it is also very modern. As it has been constructed, the supporting plastic-pipe frame is 28½ inches high, plus the thickness of the glass. Overall it is 28½ by 28 inches. The half inch is a slight error on the part of its builder. The glass top is ⅝ inch thick and 36 by 36 inches. The size is ideal for two or four diners, as well as candles and wine.

The glass remains on its frame by virtue of its weight. The glass is centered by eye; there is no need for any greater accuracy, and there is no need to fasten the glass in place. Its weight will hold it down.

Although the frame may appear to be fragile, it is not. The 1½-inch DWV pipe with an O.D. of almost 2 inches is quite rigid. The

The weight of the glass holds it in place. Nothing else is needed.

table does not vibrate when in use. And the glass cannot be easily pushed off its supporting frame. Bumping into the side of the glass will not send it sliding to the floor.

ALTERNATE APPLICATIONS Since the top is glass and the frame is plastic, the table is just about as rustproof and non-biodegradable as anything short of gold can be. Therefore it makes an excellent outdoor table. If it is used outdoors and a high wind is expected, the glass should be removed and placed on the grass. The grass will not harm the glass. Or, the glass can be covered with a thick layer of newspapers, with large rocks or concrete blocks atop the paper to hold the glass down. This is what might be done should the table be left outside all winter. The only possible natural harm that might come to the table is that a very strong wind might blow the top away.

VARIATIONS As the table now stands the top of the frame consists of three parallel crossbars. If desired, this number could be reduced to two—or increased to four. It would be unsafe to reduce pipe size. A larger pipe size, this designer believes, would make the table blocky and awkward.

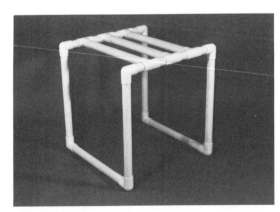

The table's supporting frame of 1½-inch DWV pipe. The legs can be removed from the balance of the frame for storage or shipment.

The same design could be reduced in all dimensions and pipe size *Size*
to make a coffee or night table, say with a 24 by 24-inch glass top.
One-inch or 1¼-inch pipe would be attractive.

The design could also be utilized to support a low-placed cushion, which would make it a hassock. A frame height of roughly 15
inches would be about right. A fourth crossbar would be needed
and the frame-top dimensions should be such as to provide suitable support for the thick cushion selected.

With a smaller glass top, it is advisable to retain the same frame
dimensions if the height remains the same. If the present frame is
reduced to much below 28 by 28 inches, it becomes too "tippy"
and unstable.

Going in the other direction, the length of the frame could be
increased a foot without problems. If the frame's length is increased beyond this figure, or if the width of the frame (the length
of the crossbars) is increased, braces should be installed all
around. Very simply, this means adding T's to each leg and connecting the legs to each other by horizontal pieces of pipe. When
this is done the frame can be extended to 6 feet by 4 feet without
any danger of the table tipping or collapsing.

The glass used in the illustrations is ⅝ inch thick. It is expensive when it is perfect, but with some searching one may find
glass that is imperfect—chipped or wavy—for a lot less. This or a
greater thickness is best for a 36-by-36 tabletop. If desired, glass
thickness can go down to ⅜ inch with reasonable safety; even
thinner glass plate can be used if the tabletop size is reduced.
Should you make the table longer, the ⅝-inch thickness must remain or be increased. If this is done, it should be remembered that
the glass pictured weighs about 75 pounds, and although that is
not a difficult weight for an adult, two people are needed to handle it safely. (It's shifting the glass from the vertical to the horizontal position that gets you.)

The dining room table can double as a coffee table. Here, the glass *Coffee*
and the supporting frame remain the same; only the legs are *table*
changed. Instead of U-shaped legs, single, straight legs are used—

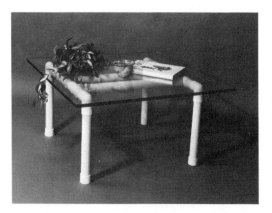

Here is the same table on short,
straight legs being used as a coffee
table.

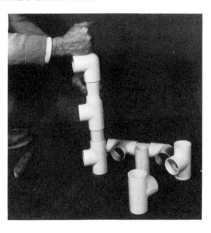

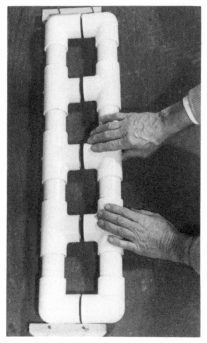

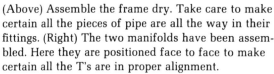

(Above) Assemble the frame dry. Take care to make certain all the pieces of pipe are all the way in their fittings. (Right) The two manifolds have been assembled. Here they are positioned face to face to make certain all the T's are in proper alignment.

15 inches or so in length—their bottom ends capped with cap fittings. Since there is no need to cement or screw-fasten the legs to the frame, it is a simple matter to withdraw one set of legs and replace them with another.

PROCEDURE   The first step is to cut the 1½-inch DWV pipe to size. Then the frame is assembled dry, with care taken to drive all the pieces of pipe all the way into their fittings.

For the sake of clarity, we shall call the sides of the frame that underlies the glass top the manifolds. The only reason for this name is that these pipe assemblies do look somewhat like the manifold on an engine. In any case, two scraps of lumber are fastened to the work board, with care taken to keep the sides of the pieces of wood parallel. A separation of 26 inches should be tried, and changed if necessary. When both manifolds have been assembled—dry—they are placed parallel to one another and facing one another between the scraps of wood. All the fittings are pressed down flat against the work board. The facing is examined, fitting ends opened. They must all line up. If they don't, the manifold must be taken apart and the necessary adjustments made. It is not important that the spacings between the T's are exactly as shown or suggested; it is not necessary that the manifolds be exactly 28½ inches long. What is necessary is that both manifolds be exactly the same length and that each T is exactly in line with its opposite T. If not, the table will not go together correctly.

The scraps of lumber are removed from the work board. The *Assembling* frame's crossbars are positioned within their respective T's in the *the frame* two manifolds. The two manifolds are forced together. This will be easier to do if a pair of guides of scrap lumber is again fastened to the work board.

When this has been done, and when measurements show that all the parts assembled form a perfect rectangle or square—all parts parallel and square—the pieces forming the frame are ready to be cemented together. *Note:* The 90-degree elbows forming the corners of the frame *are not cemented* at this time. To be certain this error is not made, the elbows should be removed from the work area.

Cementing is accomplished exactly as described in chapter 4. But there is a small variation to be suggested. If the reader is or has been a mechanical engineering student he or she will immediately realize on inspecting the design that all that keeps the table from collapsing sideways are the manifold joints. All these joints must be "solid" from end elbow to end elbow. Therefore, it is suggested that "primer" be used on each joint before the cement is applied.

The primer is a water-thin liquid suitable for both PVC and CPVC. It is applied with a small brush to the inside of the fitting and to the outer surface of the pipe end. Then the cement is applied and the two pieces are joined. The primer softens the plastic, helping the cement do its job. When a primer-cement joint hardens there is no way the two pieces of plastic can be separated. They have been welded together.

This sounds wonderful and it is. However, there is one draw-

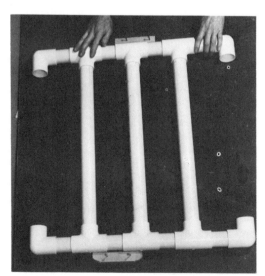

The two manifolds are temporaily joined by the cross bars. The scraps of lumber nailed to the work board serve as a jig and make assembly easier.

back. In addition to its cost, the primer has a tremendous urge to run and drip. Where it drips it stains. Thus just enough and no more must be applied. And the frame should be assembled upside down so that stains resulting from runs and drips end up on the underside of the table. All that can be done with a stain is cut it off with a razor; it is permanent. Yet the primer does slow the setting of the cement a little, which helps.

In cementing the parts of the frame together, four right-angle guides are prepared on the work board. The guides are positioned so as to contain or hold the assembled frame together. The assembled frame is turned on its back and disassembled, a piece at a time. Any corner is suitable to begin work—by cementing one nipple (short piece of pipe) into its T. The nipple is driven into place before the cement hardens. One crossbar is inserted into the T without cement. *The crossbar remains dry at this time.* The following nipple is cemented into place and then driven home. The second nipple is followed by the second T. This T is attached dry to its crossbar. Now the second T is cemented and driven into place. The reason for all this is that it is vital that the T's be parallel and in line; otherwise the crossbars will not fit, or the frame will be crooked.

When the manifolds have been assembled and cemented, the cement should be allowed an hour or so to harden fully. Then, the crossbars are ready to be cemented to the manifolds. One after another, all three bars are cemented to one manifold. Cement alone can be used; there is no need for maximum joint strength here. To cement the three bar ends to the remaining manifold takes a bit of doing. Cement dries fast and all three pipe ends must get into the fittings almost simultaneously. This craftsperson suggests a dry run first; then cement can be applied to the

(Left) Here the nipples are being cemented to the T's. Note that the cross bars remain dry at this time, and that the elbows at the ends of the manifolds are not cemented at this time.

(Right) The three cross bars have been cemented to one manifold. Now a dry run is being made to see how well the cross bars will fit into the second manifold.

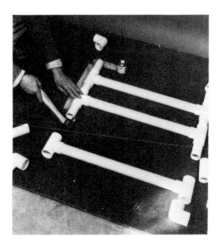

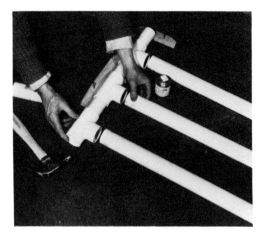

Cement is placed on the ends of the three cross bars. Now the three bars must be forced into their respective T's simultaneously. At the same time, the entire frame must be held flat against the work board.

pipe ends and all three of them driven home simultaneously. The entire frame should be held flat against the work board for a few minutes, to ensure that the frame will be flat when the job is done.

   Note: If the frame is to have short legs and be used for a coffee table, there is no need to cement the crossbars; friction alone will hold them in place, or they can be fastened with screws. Screws can also hold the bars for a "full" table; it will be safe enough, although cement will make it a bit steadier.

With the frame parts all joined, the end fittings—the elbows that hold the legs—are ready to be cemented onto the frame. This is a simple cementing job, but the primer should be used, and the elbow must be held perfectly vertical until the cement sets up. It is important to bear in mind that the leg is *not cemented* to the fitting at this time.

Cementing the end fittings

Now the elbows are cemented onto the ends of the manifolds. Note the board taped to the side of the pipe and the combination square alongside of it. Only in this way can you be certain the elbow will form a perfect right angle with the frame.

First, the frame is placed top side down on the work board or bench. The leg or any piece of pipe is placed in one end-fitting. With masking tape a piece of straight stick is fastened to the leg, care being taken to see that the wood does touch the fitting. With the aid of the combination square, the leg is adjusted until it is perfectly vertical. The fitting and the frame are marked, as suggested in chapter 4. The fitting and leg or pipe are removed. The primer and then the cement are applied. The fitting on the end of the frame is replaced and driven home with a hammer. Now the fitting is turned quickly until the two marks that have been made are aligned. Then the square is quickly brought to bear and the leg given whatever final adjustment may be necessary to make it perfectly vertical. There should be a wait of at least ten minutes before going on to the next elbow fitting.

Assembling the table The pieces of pipe forming the legs and the crossbar or brace are assembled to form the two U's required. These joints can be left dry or fastened with cement or screws. The frame is placed top side down. The legs are then pressed into their respective fittings. Again the choice of leaving these joints dry, or of using screws or cement is up to the individual. The joints will hold entirely satisfactorily without any assistance.

The elbows cemented in place, you can now install the legs. None of the leg elbows need to be cemented in place or fastened with screws.

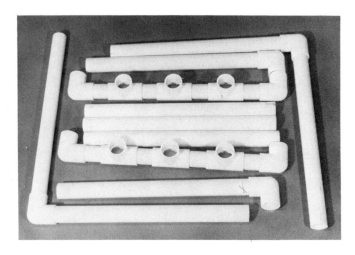

The completely disassembled dining room table. In this case the cross bars were not cemented into the manifolds. If you are leery about this, fasten the cross bars in place with screws.

DISASSEMBLY

No problem here. The glass is removed simply by lifting it up and away. Just how many pieces can be made out of the table depends on how the pieces have been joined. All manifolds and the elbows at their ends must be fully cemented on a full-size table. The crossbars and legs can be joined dry. If that is the way a reader constructs a full-size table, the accompanying illustrations shows how the table will look disassembled.

Pipe	1-inch I.D., 18 feet long, cut into:
	4 15½-inch sectons
	4 14½ sections
	2 11-inch sections
	4 10½-inch sections
	6 2-inch sections (nipples)
	½-inch I.D. (⅝-inch O.D.), 16 feet long, cut into:
	7 17-inch sections
	4 13-inch sections
Fittings	(To fit 1-inch I.D. pipe)
	8 T's
	8 90-degree elbows
Cushions	2 15 by 15 by 1½-inches, tie-ons

The side chair with low-priced, tie-on cushions and our old friend the flower or night stand alongside. Note that the center leg on the stand has been reduced to 18 inches and the balance of the support has also been changed.

13. Side Chair

A SIDE CHAIR IS, of course, simply a chair without arms, meaning that it is not an armchair. This one is very modern with straight, formal lines. It is designed to be used with the dining room table illustrated in chapter 12, but, of course, it could be used anywhere: in a child's room, in a kitchen, on a patio, or even in a sidewalk cafe.

The seat is designed to be used with cushions. As shown, with tie-on cushions 15 by 15 by 1½ inches in place, the seat itself is 18 inches high, which is about right for an average-size person.

Overall, the chair is 33½ inches high, 17 inches deep, and 18 inches wide. Size-wise, this is a minimum chair, comfortable but not generous. A large chair would have a wider and deeper seat. Seat height could be raised one inch, but no more. There would

The side chair without cushions.

be no need to raise the height of the back except for appearance, if desired.

Many design variations stemming from this basic design are easily made. The same chair is used as the basis of an armchair, which is described and illustrated in the next chapter.

VARIATIONS

The chair shown utilizes 1-inch pipe. One could get by with ¾-inch pipe, at a minimum, but it would be absolutely necessary to fasten all the joints, one way or another. However, if the size of the chair were reduced—to make a child's chair, for example—there would be no problem with the ¾-inch pipe. But if one tried to go to a smaller pipe, it would not be possible to insert the seat bars. The present seat bar I.D. is ½ inch. A smaller seat-bar diameter would be acceptable if the chair's size was accordingly. However, very few plumbing supply shops stock pipe under ½ inch I.D.

Size changes

Going in the other direction, as mentioned before, would not require a pipe-size increase, unless a lounge-type chair, with a seat depth of 20 inches or more, were constructed. For a chair of this type, 1¼-inch pipe for the frame would not appear too bulky.

Outdoors, cushions present a problem: they are not waterproof. To eliminate cushions and the need to drag them into the house every night, the number of seat bars used could be doubled. Beneath a moderately firm cushion, seven bars suffice. Without the cushion, twice as many bars will probably be needed on the seat for comfort. This means that two sets of holes will have to be

Cushion elimination

drilled in the elbows that form the front of the seat frame, and the balance of the bars spaced one inch apart. There is no need to increase the number of bars in the seat back.

Cushion change   The present cushions are 1½ inches thick. If a thinner cushion is used, chair leg height should be increased accordingly. With a thicker cushion there is no need to alter leg height until the thickness of the new cushion exceeds three inches. If the thickness of the back cushion is reduced, no change is necessary. If this cushion's thickness is increased, the front-to-rear measurements of the chair should be increased proportionately.

If one is uncertain of just how much should be added to the chair's dimensions because it is not known how the cushions may compress under one's weight or how the chair will feel when one sits on it, the parts should be made larger than suggested. They can always be cut down as necessary.

Design changes   The chair illustrated does not lend itself to many design or shape changes. Of course, altering its size or the size of one of its parts does constitute a shape change. But the only major change that evolves naturally from the presented design is an armchair.

If desired, the positions of the braces can be altered. The braces are the two bars in the seat frame that hold the legs together. Now, the front bar is high, while the rear bar is low. This could be reversed. The rear brace and its two T's could even be eliminated without much loss of strength. But the front brace must remain or the chair will come apart when used.

The height of the chair's back could be raised to give it a more formal appearance. And when this is done another horizontal bar could be added to the back. The back could also be angled a bit by using 22½-degree angles in the back's frame. These would be positioned just above the two T's that join the seat frame.

Hassock   If the back of the chair were eliminated and elbows utilized at the rear of the seat frame as those used at the front of the frame one would have a high hassock, or a stool. To make the conventional hassock, the legs would be shortened to make the top of the seat about fourteen inches high.

PROCEDURE   The pipe is cut into the sections suggested in the parts list at the beginning of the chapter. The seat bars and the four back bars are grouped in two separate bundles. All the other pieces are identified by size. If one writes within an inch of the pipe ends, the notations will be covered by the fitting. The reason for marking the pipe is simply that it is easy to become confused otherwise.

There are two of these 1-inch pipe bars. Each is 14½ inches long. *Seat-side*
Each is drilled to accept six ½-inch pipe ends—the seat bars. (If *bars*
they were flat they would be called slats.)

With scrap lumber a large square is made on the work board.
The two pieces of pipe are positioned within the square so that
the two pipes are parallel and their ends are in line with one another. Now, with the aid of the ruler, a pencil line is drawn down
the length of each pipe. Starting at the end of one pipe, 1½ inches
are measured off. A mark is made on the pencil line. Now 2 inches
are measured off and another mark made. This is repeated until
there are six marks. With the help of the square, each mark is
carried directly across to the line on the second pipe; mark the
second pipe as this is being done.

Some cardboard is wrapped around one of the seat-side bars
and locked in the vise. Now a pilot hole is drilled through each of
the six marks, and followed with a ⅝-inch Speedbor bit. Next,
each hole is cleaned up by just touching a countersink to it. It is
necessary only to remove the fuzz; the size of the hole should not
be changed. Now the same is done with the second seat-side bar.

Now a hole is drilled in the 90-degree elbows that terminate the

(Left) The holes that have to be cut in the pipe forming the sides of the seat are best laid out simultaneously. The cleats or guides hold the pipes in line
and parallel. Measure 1½ inches from the pipe ends
and then 2 inches, again and again to mark the centers
of the seven holes you will drill.

(Below, left) Drilling the holes in the seat sides. Drill
all the pilot holes first. Follow with the Speedbor bit
and then clean up each hole with the countersink.
(Below, right) Drilling the pilot hole in the elbow. The
elbow is held on a scrap piece of pipe. When the vise
applies pressure the pipe is distorted and holds the
elbow tightly. Note where the pilot hole is drilled, followed, of course, by the ⅝-inch bit.

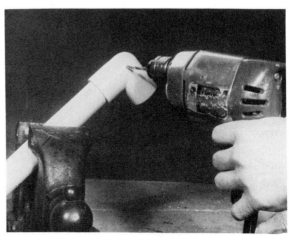

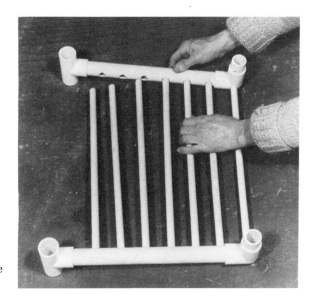

Installing the seat bars (½-inch pipe) in the holes drilled in the sides of the seat.

front end of the seat-side bars. A piece of scrap pipe is placed in the vise. One of the elbows is placed on the pipe. Now the pressure on the pipe is tightened by tightening the vise. This will, more or less, expand the pipe and lock the elbow in place. Next, a pilot hole is drilled into the elbow. This hole should be centered in the corner of the fitting. A line should be drawn—or visualized—that connects the inside corner of the fitting with its outside corner, and the exact center of this line should be drilled. The pilot hole is enlarged with the ⅝-inch Speedbor bit and cleaned up with a touch of the countersink bit. Of course, two such holes are needed in two elbows.

T's are slipped onto the rear ends of the two seat-side bars and the drilled elbows onto the front ends of the same two bars. (The seat bar holes start closer to the front of the seat-side bars than to their rear ends.) Now the 17-inch-long, ⅝-inch-O.D. seat bars are placed on the work board and slipped into the holes in the seat-side bars. It will be noted that the seat bars are shorter than their alloted spaces. This makes it easier to get the bars into place. When this task has been completed, the nipples (2-inch pipe) can be cemented into the elbows. The seat will be assembled and disassembled from the balance of the chair at this point, but there is no need for the nipple to be loose in both fittings.

Legs and braces   The legs and braces are assembled dry, then measured or sized, and tried for fit. This is done by simply fitting the seat onto the legs and forcing all the pipes all the way into the joints. When this has been done the seat and legs can be checked with the rule to make certain everything is square and shipshape. If all is well

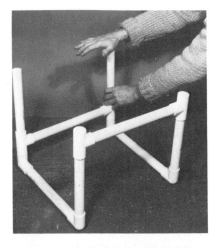

(Top left) Assembling the chair's bottom frame. (Top, right) The seat is positioned atop the bottom frame.

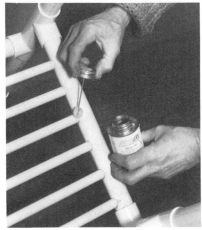

(Left) The chair is turned on its back and a dab of cement is applied to each joint. The cement keeps the seat bars from sliding to and fro.

these parts can remain "dry," or some or all of them can be cemented together. For easy disassembly, the legs are separated from the T's. The legs are then cemented to the right-angle elbows that go on their bottoms and the pipe that fits into the elbows. The result is a pair of U's. The braces are cemented to their T's; one must make certain the T's are parallel. Now, if desired, the seat bars can be cemented fast to the seat-side bars. The seat is simply turned over and a few drops of cement placed on the outside of the joint between the seat bars and the supporting pipe. Some of the cement will seep into the joint and lock the bar in place. Since there is no load on these bars, that is all that is necessary.

The two horizontal pipes that will be drilled for the seat-back bars are marked off, in the same way the seat-side bars were marked off. The back has only four bars. The back bars are 13 inches long. The drilled pipes that hold the back bars in a vertical

Seat back

(Left) Assembling the seat back.

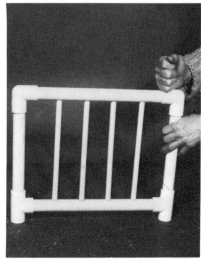

(Right) The top bar on the seat back is driven into place.

You can either cement the parts of the seat back together or join them with screws, as shown.

position are 15½ inches long. The first ⅝-inch hole is centered exactly 3½ inches from either pipe end. The next hole is exactly 3 inches away, and so on for a total of four holes.

When the back bars have been inserted in their holes, all the pieces of pipe are forced all the way into the fittings. Then, all the joints can either be locked with screws or taken apart and cemented. If they are cemented, it should be remembered that there will be two joints that will have to be cemented simultaneously. Nothing need be done to the ⅝-inch back bars.

Assembly Now there is nothing to do but cement a nipple into each upper end of the T's forming the back of the seat. The other half of the nipple enters the lower end of the T forming the back of the chair. Cementing half of the nipple into its fitting helps keep the joint rigid, yet does not interfere with its disassembly.

Whether any of the other joints are fastened or not, these two side joints should be cemented: The nipple going downward into the T and the seat's side bar where it enters the same T. If you don't the back of the seat will rock a little.

The chair can be disassembled into six sections, each relatively flat. One is the seat, another is the back, and the remaining sections are the legs and leg braces. Of course, all the joints can remain free, but unless the chair must be packed into a minimum space, there is not much to be gained by breaking it down into forty-five separate pieces of plastic pipe.

DISASSEMBLY

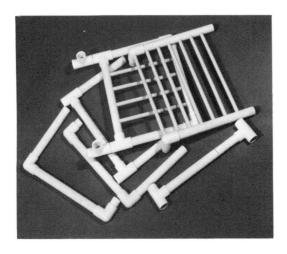

The disassembled side chair. Note tha the seat and the back have not been disassembled because it is too much of a nuisance to reassemble these parts again.

Pipe   1-inch I.D., 20 feet long, cut into:
4 15½-inch sections
4 10½-inch sections
4 11½-inch sections
2 8-inch sections
2 5½-inch sections
2 15-inch sections
14 2-inch sections (nipples)

½-inch I.D., 18 feet long cut into:
8 17-inch sections
4 13-inch sections

Fittings   (To fit 1-inch I.D. pipe)
12 T's
14 90-degree elbows

Cushions   2 15 by 15 by 1½-inches, tie-ons

Fit for a princess or at least a prince, this arm chair is a brother to the side chair illustrated previously.

14. Arm Chair

THE ARMCHAIR is a brother—or sister, if one prefers—to the side chair illustrated and described in the previous chapter. The pair, arm, and side have been designed to be used together along with the glass-topped dining room table discussed in chapter 12. Altogether they make for an ultra-modern or high-tech ensemble that is quite striking indoors or out.

As can readily be seen, the armchair is exactly the same as the side chair, which brings them visually into harmony. The difference is the addition of the arms.

The arm chair is 34¼ inches high, 25¾ inches wide overall. It has been designed for the same size cushions, 15 by 15 by 1½ inches, as used on the side chair. Seat depth is 17 inches; width is 18 inches—again, just like the side chair.

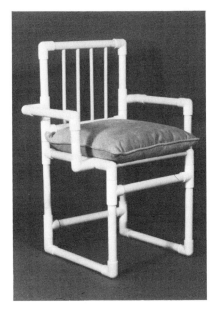
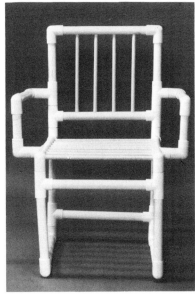

(Left) With single cushion.

(Right) The arm chair without its cushions. As you can see, it is the side chair with arms added.

The same size pipe, one-inch I.D., is used for the frame, and the same half-inch I.D. pipe is used for the seat and back bars. In the armchair, however, there are eight seat bars instead of seven. The back bars remain the same.

The only dimensional difference in the chair's frame is in shorter pieces of pipe for the seat-side and the vertical sides of the back. This is done to accommodate the T's needed to hold the chair's arms.

VARIATIONS

Size

The same size variations suggested previously apply here. The armchair's seat can be made a little wider, deeper, and higher, if desired, so long as the cushion is accounted for, and the general size remains within the limits comfortable to the human frame.

One might wish to hold all the dimensions and just raise the back of the chair. That would make it somewhat more formal, and in some instances, armchairs are a bit higher in the back than side chairs.

Design

A major design change easily adapted to the armchair shown can be made by changing the arms. As constructed, the arms begin at T's incorporated into the sides of the chair's back, go outward, and then forward, down, and back inward to rejoin the sides of the seat frame. Because we are forced to use existing fittings, each arm's center moves outward from the chair's sides by close to 4 inches, bringing the chair's overall width to 25¾ inches. Some sitters will find this armspread just right; others may find it a bit too wide. In any case, if one is tight for space and still wants an arm chair, the arms can be fastened by another means or arrangement.

The photo of the armchair should be examined, with note taken of how the arms are positioned at present. Now mentally (or physically, if one is in the process of assembling the chair) the arm should be removed, the top T swung forward, and the lower T upwards. Now the arm comes directly forward from the upper T and then turns down to join the lower T. This design will save two elbows on each arm. It will also reduce the chair's overall width by some eight inches. However, the average male will find the chair constricting. (Fatties won't be able to get into it.) If this design is used, the horizontal pieces of pipe should be increased by two inches in length. This will make the chair two inches wider. The same cushions can still be used, if desired. Everything else remains the same except the holes for the back bars. The first hole will have to be four-and-one-fourth inches in from the end of the pipe.

If one decides to make the chair two inches wider and remove the bends in the arms, some part changes and one construction change will have to be made. Part change and construction change are discussed at the end of this chapter.

PROCEDURE   As one will probably start with two 10-foot pieces of 1-inch pipe, it will probably be best to measure up the pipe before it is cut into sections. The 20 necessary feet given include a little less than 1½ feet to spare, but if one errs in dividing the pipe into sections, it is easy to end up with too many short pieces.

Once the pipe has been cut into sections, lots of time searching and fitting will be saved if like-size pieces are placed in groups and each group marked. It is easy to mix the 10½-inch pieces and the 11½-inch pieces together. No harm done, but it is a nuisance changing them around.

To ease assembly, each nipple is cemented into one of the two fittings it will join.

Making   Each seat-side bar consists of an elbow, connected by a nipple to
the seat   a T, which in turn is connected to an 11½-inch piece of 1-inch I.D. pipe. There are, of course, two seat-side bars. Both are assembled dry. A cleat—a piece of scrap lumber—is fastened to the work board. The two seat-side bars are aligned, side by side, T's pointing away from each other, elbows down and against the cleat. Now 3 inches from the front of the seat bars are measured off with a ruler and pencil; a mark is made on the top of the pipes. Two inches more are measured off; a second mark is made, and so on down the length of the pipe.

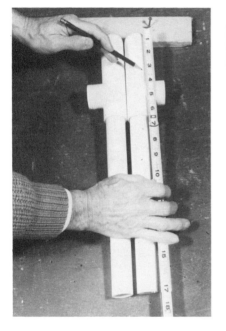

(Left) The seat-side bars are inserted in the T's, connected to the front-of-the seat elbows and placed on the work board side by side. Here, the hole centers for the seat bars are measured off. The first center is 3 inches from the front of the seat. The next is 2 inches farther along and so on. (Above) One seat-side bar and its front fittings are held in your vise. Now the hole centers for the seat bar marks are carried down the side of the fittings. The first hole goes in the diagonal center of the elbow.

One marked and assembled seat-side bar is placed in the vise, the elbow projecting down. With a square, the marks are transferred to the side of the pipe. Then a line is drawn down the length of the pipe, along its center. Another line is drawn along the fold in the elbow—a fine line will be seen there. Where the lines or marks cross is where pilot holes will be drilled. In all, eight holes will be located and drilled in each seat-side bar. The first is centered 1 inch in from the end of the elbow, the second 3 inches in from the end of the elbow, the third 2 inches from the second hole, and so on.

With the pilot holes drilled in the seat-side bars, the holes are now ready to be enlarged with the ⅝-inch Speedbor bit. But be-

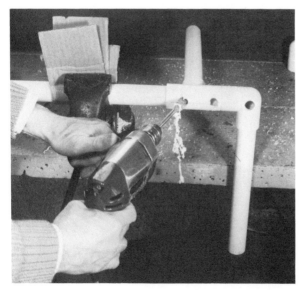

Pilot holes have been drilled into the seat-side bar. Now the holes are enlarged to ⅝ inch with the Speedbor bit. The pieces of pipe in the fittings are there temporarily to make certain the fittings are properly aligned with each other.

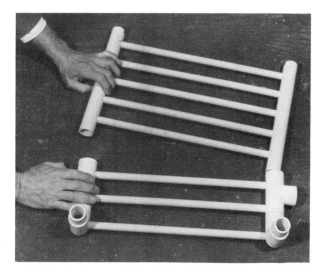

The seat bars have been inserted in the seat-side bars and fittings. Now the parts are assembled to form the seat proper.

fore this is done, it is necessary to make certain that the open end of the elbow points straight down, and that the opening in the T that adjoins it points straight out, which is to say that it is exactly horizontal. It is difficult to determine with any degree of accuracy just where a fitting may be pointing, so we insert short pieces of pipe temporarily in each fitting. This makes it easy to check on the angle of the fitting, and for maximum accuracy we can apply the level—which is incorporated into most combination squares—to each piece of pipe.

The fittings pointed in the correct direction, we can now drill the seat-side bars to make holes to accept the ends of the seat bars. It may be noted that the only difference in this portion of the construction of the armchair from that of the side chair is that there is a T fitting in the seat-side bars.

Next, the seat bars are slipped into the seat-side bars. In other words, the seat itself is assembled. All this is done dry, of course. Nothing beyond the nipples is cemented or screwed fast into place as yet. The seat can be assembled in sections as shown, or all at once, as was done in the previous project.

Seat frame With the seat assembled, the seat frame can now be assembled. No problem here, since it is impossible to mix up the parts permanently. When the seat and the supporting frame have been assembled, the seat is turned on its back and sides and a person's weight put on it to make certain that all the pipes have been forced all the way into their respective fittings. Even if one never wishes to disassemble the arm chair, it is inadvisable to fasten any of the joints as yet.

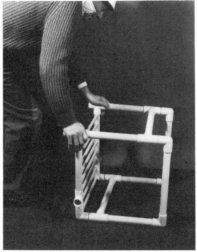

(Left) The entire seat frame is now assembled. Note the direction in which the T's that hold the chair's arms are pointing.

(Right) Turn the seat frame over several times and press down on it to make certain all the pipe ends have entered the fittings as far as they can go.

The seat back consists of two horizontal pieces of pipe, each 15½ inches long. Each pipe is drilled four times to provide four ⅝-inch holes for the vertical back bars. The first hole is centered 3¼ inches from either end of the pipe, the following hole 3 inches, center to center, farther along and so on, which leaves 3¼ inches from the center of the last hole to the end of the pipe. The vertical back bars are cut from ½-inch I.D. stock, and are 13 inches long. The vertical sides of the back frame consist of two lengths of 1-inch pipe, 8 inches long, joined by nipples to two T's. One T (on one side) holds the end of the seat arm. The second T, directly underneath, comprises the bottom corner of the seat back and joins the T on the upper corner of the seat frame. In any case, all this should be clear on viewing the illustrations. It is necessary to make certain that the back of the chair is securely and fully inserted into the fittings on top of the seat frame.

Making the seat back

(Left) Assemble the back of the seat; force all the pipe ends into their fittings. Note the direction the T's are pointing.

(Right) Connect the seat back to the seat frame.

Making the armrests The armrest begins with an elbow that is connected to the side of the back with a nipple. The elbow holds the arm itself, which is an 11½-inch length of 1-inch pipe. This goes to an elbow facing down, which accepts a 5½-inch length of the same pipe. Then there is another elbow that is coupled to the T in the seat-side bar with a nipple.

All this is simple enough assembly. If the joints don't fit properly, if things do not look reasonably shipshape, an error has probably been made in cutting the pipe to length. We say "reasonably shipshape" because on completing the illustrated armchair we found two pieces of pipe almost one inch oversize—which is to say that perfection is not absolutely necessary. The error in pipe lengths was hardly noticeable. However, there are two places where near perfection is a must. These are the joints between the arms and the T's in the seat-side bars. If these T's do not poke out perfectly horizontally, the chair immediately looks crooked.

So, the chair should be turned over several times and all the joints pressed firmly home. Then the chair is righted and that oft-mentioned piece of straight board placed across the arms of the chair. Then the aforementioned joints should be viewed against this piece of wood from a reflective distance. Any inaccuracies in the joints will immediately be obvious. The necessary adjustments are made: the T ends raised or lowered until they are perfectly horizontal. Next, a 7/64-inch pilot hole is drilled through the T fitting and into the underlying pipe. A short nail is forced into the hole. If the nail sits loosely, it should be bent a little before it is forced into place. Doing this locks the T fitting in place. This is done to both T fittings, the chair is turned over and the same T fittings are screw-fastened to their respective pipes. The nails are removed, and the holes filled with putty if desired.

(Left) Now the chair's arms are connected.

(Right) Once again the pipes are pressed tightly into their fittings.

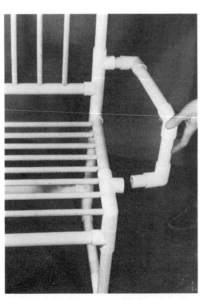
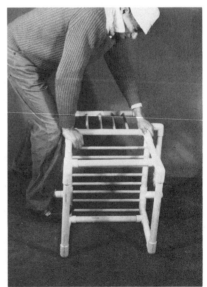

 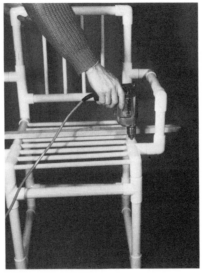

(Left) That familiar straight piece of wood is placed across the arms of the chair. Using this straight "edge" as a guide, the T's holding the arms are adjusted until they are parallel with the edge.

(Right) A pilot hole is drilled through the T's and a nail is pushed into each hole to lock the T's in place. Following, the chair is turned over and the same fitting is permanently joined to its pipe with a screw. The nail can then be removed and the hole filled with a little putty.

An alternative method to locking the same T's in perfect position without leaving visible holes is to turn the chair on its back, use the piece of wood to align the T's, and then drill for screws. This method saves drilling the nail holes, but this craftsperson believes the first method produces more accurate results.

If one wishes, only the two joints mentioned must be locked firm, one way or another. The chair holds fairly straight and tight without any of the other joints being locked. However, the back will flex a bit unless a few more joints are premanently locked. Specifically, the two T's on each side of the back should be locked to the balance of the back frame. But neither the arms nor the back frame as a whole have to be fastened to the adjoining parts.

DISASSEMBLY

Here's the chair in its knocked down state. Note that neither the seat nor the back is taken apart.

Joined only at these points, the armchair can be broken down into back section, seat section, arms, and leg parts.

DESIGN AND SIZE CHANGE If it is decided to make the chair wider and to remove the bends from its arms, thus making its overall width narrower, the following parts changes are made, and shown here.

> *1-inch pipe:*
> > *change 4 15½-inch sections to 17½ inches.*
> > *4 2-inch sections are eliminated.*
> *½-inch pipe:*
> > *total length is increased to 20 feet.*
> > *8 17-inch sections are changed to 19 inches.*
> *Fittings (to fit 1-inch I.D. pipe)*
> > *4 90-degree elbows are eliminated.*

Procedure change In the illustrated armchair the seat-side arms have two T's. Each T protrudes outward and horizontally from the seat-side bar. In this version of the armchair, these two T's point directly upward. (The elbows at the ends of the same pipes point directly downward.) Thus the seat bar holes are drilled into the sides of the T's. Assembly is exactly the same.

The book case in use.

PARTS LIST/BOOK CASE

Wood	¾-inch chipboard or plywood; 3 pieces, 48 by 14 inches
Pipe	1-inch PVC, 28 feet long, cut into:
	2 37-inch sections
	6 14½-inch sections
	4 13-inch sections
	4 12-inch sections
	2 10-inch sections
	2 6½-inch sections
	4 4-inch sections
	2 2-inch sections
	2 3-inch sections
Fittings	To accept 1-inch PVC pipe
	16 T's
	8 caps
Screws	12 2-inch #10 flathead wood screws

15. Bookcase

T HE THREE-SHELF BOOKCASE illustrated is made of 1-inch PVC pipe and ¾-inch chipboard. Overall it stands 50 inches high, is 48 inches wide, and 18 inches deep. The separation between shelves is 13 and 14 inches. The separation was varied not only to permit objects of differing heights to be placed on the shelves, but to make the visual aspect of the bookcase a bit more interesting.

As shown, the bookcase has two horizontal braces. This makes it fairly rigid. Just one could suffice, saving some pipe and fittings, but the case would shake a bit.

Chipboard was selected for the shelves because it has a pleasant brown color, and because it has no grain and will not warp. However, chipboard is very heavy and will gradually sag if it is loaded

VARIATIONS

123

The book case with empty shelves. Here you can see how a brace has been positioned atop the rear legs.

too heavily. To keep the chipboard from becoming stained with time it is advisable to give it a coat or two of clear lacquer or varnish.

Other shelving Surprisingly, ordinary pine shelving boards cost more than chipboard unless 10-inch or narrower boards are used. If wood shelving is chosen, number 2 lumber—which has small, tight knots—should be used. Number 3, which is scarce today, is much cheaper but has large, loose knots. Some of the lumberyards and even hardware shops carry prefinished shelving. These boards are more expensive but they save you the trouble of finishing.

Plywood is also useful for these shelves, but it has two drawbacks. First, ¾-inch plywood with a visually attractive surface is expensive. Very likely the entire 4-by-8-foot sheet will have to be purchased before the yard will cut it for the buyer. Also, plywood has a raw edge. It must either be hidden with a strip of wood or sanded carefully down and sealed with several coats of shellac followed by varnish. Some craftspeople paint the ends of plywood panels to hide the grain.

Size The bookcase can be made in any size, and with as many shelves as desired. However, if chipboard is used for the shelving it is inadvisable to space the supports more than 38 inches apart, which we have done in the example. But there is no reason why the bookcase cannot have three pairs of legs, nor any reason why there cannot be more shelves. The only restriction, assuming the bookcase is to stand free, is that its top shelf be held to a maximum of 60 inches above the floor, and the depth of the case kept at 14 inches or more. At this height, it is advisable to install four braces. The horizontal bars running across the width of the case brace it. If the bookcase is fitted into an alcove or fastened to a wall, it can be built up to the ceiling. The pipe will handle a tremendous compressive load without problems.

The 1-inch pipe selected is about minimum for this project. On the other hand, there is nothing to be gained by using larger-diameter pipe, except for, perhaps, a more pleasing appearance, or if one is seeking to eliminate most of the fittings and thus cut cost.

Design

The shelf-to-supporting-pipe joint is a simple lay-on joint. Wood screws coming up through the bottom of the pipe lock the boards in place. This is the simplest, easiest way of handling this portion of the construction. However, as one can imagine, there are alternatives. The best consists of using 1¼- or 1½-inch DWV pipe for the legs and fastening each shelf to the legs by means of cross-pipe joints. Obviously four such joints will be needed for each shelf, which with three shelves totals 12 joints. This is not too difficult to do if all the legs are aligned in a jig that holds them parallel, and the cuts are then made across four legs (pipes) at one time. If this is done, care should be taken to make the completed cut (opening) a hair's breadth smaller than the board so that the board has to be forced into place. If the joint fit is loose, the case will shake.

Should these joints be very loose or should considerable rigidity be desired, four horizontal braces should be applied, with one or two diagonal braces then added if necessary. This can be done by securing four 45-degree T's. The T's are inserted within the leg pipes—two to a leg. One T faces up and the other down. When pipes are cemented within these T's, the cross brace will make the bookcase rock-steady.

PROCEDURE

First, the pipe is cut up and the pieces placed in groups according to size. The shelving is secured.

*Making
the supports*

The supports consist of pieces of pipe that terminate in T's. They go beneath the shelves, which they support. To start, one end of each of the six 14½-inch pieces of pipe is cemented to a T. It is

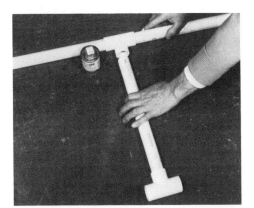

Cementing the support bars to their respective T's. The legs have been inserted in the T only to help make certain it is parallel with the work board underneath.

important to make certain that the pipe goes all the way into the T. Next, the second T must be cemented to the other end of the same pipe. To do this, two pieces of pipe—any pieces of pipe—are first positioned within the ends of the T. Then the cement is applied and the support-bar end forced into the T; one must make certain that the two pieces of pipe are flat against the work board, and that the cemented-in-place T is also flat against the same work board. This is done to all the six supports.

Fastening the supports On the underside of each shelf, near its end, a line is drawn 4½ inches in from the end and parallel to that end. Each support will be centered above one of these lines.

The end of one shelf is raised on a piece of scrap lumber. One support is positioned above the line on that shelf end. Now three pilot holes are drilled through the pipe and into the shelf. The combination square is used to make certain that the T's attached to the support bar are perfectly vertical. A 5/32-inch twist drill is used. The holes are centered on the line that has been drawn, and care is taken not to drill more than one-half inch into the shelf. The spacing between the three holes is not critical unless one wants all six support bars to be interchangeable, in which case all the holes must be spaced exactly the same distance apart. The easier way is simply to mark the bottom of each support bar and its location. Then, should the bars be removed, they can always be returned easily to their proper location.

In any event, when the pilot holes have been drilled, 3/16-inch clearance holes are drilled through the pipe. This is followed with the countersink to permit the screw's head to rest below the surface of the pipe.

The next step, of course, is to fasten the support bars to their shelves with 2-inch #10 flathead wood screws.

Now the nipples and each short piece of pipe can be cemented to one fitting. If on completion the bookcase shakes a little too

(Left) Each support bar is centered over a line drawn 4½ inches in from the ends of the shelves.

(Right) The shelf is lifted up on a piece of scrap lumber. Pilot holes are driven through the support bar and into the shelving. Use a 5/32-inch pilot drill and drive it no more than ½ inch into the ¾-inch chipboard shelving.

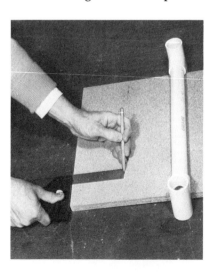

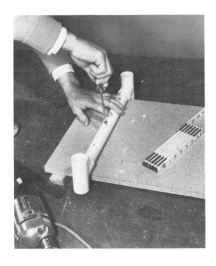

(Left) Drill 3/16-inch clearance holes through the pipe and countersink the holes. Then drive 2-inch #10 flat head screws through the pipe and into the shelving. Three screws per support bar is plenty.

(Right) Cement the short pieces of pipe into their fittings. With a hammer tap them firmly into place.

much, all the fittings can be cemented together, but that, of course, will join the parts permanently and disassembly will never be possible.

First, the caps are placed on the ends of the legs. If the caps are loose, a dab of cement will hold them in place. If there are braces, the legs should be inserted in the T's attached to the braces. This is followed by inserting whatever nipples or short legs may be necessary to support the first shelf. With the first shelf in place, the four legs that support the second shelf are inserted, the second shelf is positioned, and so on up to the top. The final step will depend on whether or not there is a rear brace only or a front and rear brace. In any case, it is a simple matter of assembly.

Assembly

For most applications, the two horizontal braces shown in the first photos are all that are needed. Except for cementing half of each nipple to its fitting and cementing the fittings on the ends of the braces to the braces, all the other joints can remain dry. How-

(Left) A close-up of the rear brace and its leg.

(Right) Assembling the balance of the book case.

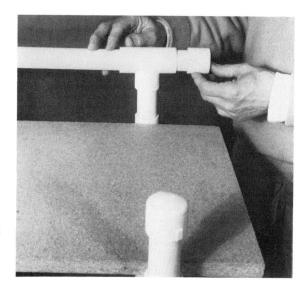

This T fitting and cap can be replaced by an elbow. It will be just as strong. In either design, the brace should be cemented to the fitting at its end.

ever, if the bookcase is going to be heavily loaded and there is concern that it may start going sideways and keep on going, four screws should be used at each shelf end. If there is still reason for concern, the diagonal bracing should be installed as suggested. The ends of these braces must be cemented or screwed fast to their respective fittings if they are to be at all effective.

DISASSEMBLY No problem—just a matter of taking the bookshelf apart. Unless there is very little space within which to fit the parts, the support bars can be left screwed fast.

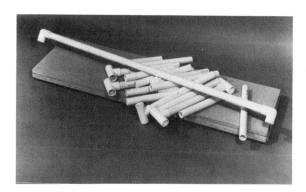

The disassembled bookcase. This is an early model with just a single rear brace terminating in two elbows.

Chaise with "standard" cushion, flower-side up.

PARTS LIST/CHAISE LOUNGE

Pipe	1-inch I.D., 32 feet long cut into:
	8 17¾-inch sections
	2 34-inch sections
	2 13-inch sections
	4 11-inch sections
	6 7-inch sections
	2 5-inch sections
	6 4-inch sections
	6 2-inch sections (nipples)
Fittings	(For 1-inch I.D. pipe)
	8 90-degree elbows
	4 45-degree elbows
	16 T's
Cushion	68½ by 23½ inches; 2½ or more inches thick

16. Chaise Lounge

THE CHAISE LOUNGE pictured at the beginning of this book is one of our early chaise designs. We used ¾-inch I.D. pipe with steel plus concrete (actually cement) to reinforce the 45-degree elbow (joint) between the back and seat portions of the chaise. At this writing, the chaise has been left to the weather for three years. Neither rain, snow, nor sub-zero temperature has affected it, though no one has sat on it during the winter. (Plastic is very brittle when it becomes very cold.) If one elects to construct this chaise, the rear legs should be moved back toward the rear of the frame a few inches, with another support bar or two added. There is a bit too much space between these bars; the cushion tends to sink between them. The chaise described and illustrated here incorporates what we have learned about plastic-pipe furniture since then.

Chaise frame alone viewed, more or less, from its front end.

The improved chaise design utilizes one-inch I.D. pipe without internal reinforcement. The new design derives its strength from advanced engineering techniques, at least as applied to furniture construction. A careful look at the side view will show that both the front and rear legs tilt outward from the vertical. This has been done to put a tension on the frame, pushing its center up and giving it a slight but visible curve. When someone is on the chaise, body weight pushes downward on the frame and acts to pull the legs together and into a vertical direction. In other words, the frame is constructed much like a bridge that has an upward curve in its middle. A load on the bridge pushes down against the curve. If the bridge were perfectly flat the weight of trucks and cars pushing down on its middle would bend the bridge down in its middle. This would result in a pulling action that would be much harder to resist than a pushing action.

The end result is a curved, springy chaise that can carry a 300-pound person without complaint. However, it will not withstand the same person bouncing up and down, as this can bring the load to more than 1,000 pounds. Neither can it withstand a pile of kids

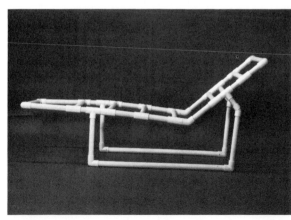

Side view of chaise frame. Note curve in frame's side and the angle of its legs.

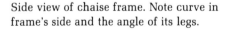

jumping up and down. If one expects marauding kids it is advisable to brace the legs. This is done by introducing T's into each leg and tying the legs on one side of the chaise to the legs on the other side of the chaise with pieces of pipe. (This is the way the front and rear of the side chair and the armchair are braced.)

As it now stands or lies, the chaise is 61 inches long, overall, 27 inches high at its highest point, 12½ inches high at its lowest point, and 21 inches wide. It has been made for a cushion or pad 68½ inches long, 23½ inches wide, and 2½ inches thick. The cushion overhangs the frame by 1¼ inches on each side and about the same at the ends. If this last figure appears in error, it should be remembered that the seat portion of the chaise is 42 inches long and the back 24 inches long—as measured from the center of the 45-degree elbow. This makes for a total of 66 inches, which would leave a total of 2½ inches of overhang, but some of the length of the cushion is lost at the fold.

The chaise frame has been deliberately made smaller than its cushion. The overhang helps keep the cushion in place. The alternative would require at least double the number of support bars than now used to keep the cushion from falling through the frame.

Some of the lounges designed to be used outdoors today are made to accommodate two persons at once. To convert the present design to a two-man or a two-woman or a heterosexual chaise would require increasing its width accordingly. The same size pipe could be used. However, a total of twelve support bars would be needed in place of the present eight, plus a pair of side-to-side braces connecting the legs, and two more long braces connecting the legs on the same side. Each of these braces would be positioned high up on the legs so the long second brace would almost touch the underside of the frame side. Thus, when the chaise was loaded, the frame sides would rest on the side braces. In this way the number of frame sides would be doubled.

An alternative can be to use larger pipe; 1½-inch DWV would be fine. But more support bars would still be needed as suggested, plus the braces that go beneath the frame from leg to leg.

Instead of two legs on each side connected by a long brace, three or more legs terminated with caps could be installed. The frame could be extended up and over the back section and used to support a canvas sunshade.

If desired, arms could be added to the chaise, using the same arrangement of parts used on the armchair.

VARIATIONS

Size

Design

PROCEDURE   First, the cushion is obtained. Although it is purchased from stock from a large department store, it may not be available everywhere. Assuming a cushion of this size can be acquired, fine; the 1-inch pipe can now be cut into the lengths indicated. If a cushion this size is not available, the frame parts' dimensions must be adjusted accordingly. The way to do this is to draw a rectangle on the work board, the same size as the cushion, and then draw another rectangle within it. A space 1½ inches wide is left between the sides of the inner and outer rectangles. The outer rectangle is erased, and the inner rectangle should be exactly equal to the overall dimensions of the frame. All the necessary fittings are placed in their proper positions within the rectangle. The spacing between fitting ends is measured. Exactly 1⅛ inches of pipe are allowed for each fitting opening. The pipe is cut to these dimensions. To avoid waste, one piece of pipe should be cut at a time and the frame assembled as each piece is ready.

It should be noted that the front leg is centered 19 inches from the front end of the chaise. The center of the 45-degree elbow that divides the seat from the back is centered 42 inches back from the front end of the chaise. The rear leg is centered—that is to say, its T is centered 12½ inches from the rear of the chaise. None of these dimensions are critical. However, the two frame sides must be alike. If they are not, the support bars will not be parallel and the chances are that the chaise itself will not sit flat on the ground. (But it will still be strong and useful.)

Assembling the frames   It is very important that both frames be assembled dry, because it is very easy to become confused. As we have stated many times previously, a cementing error remains a cementing error. There is no way to open a cemented joint.

Pipe and fitting sequence runs this way: Starting at the foot of the chaise: 90-degree elbow; 11-inch piece; support T; 4-inch

(Left) Assemble the frame sides dry. Drive all the pieces of pipe fully into their fittings.

(Right) One frame side has been assembled dry. Note how the two legs and their T's are positioned at right angles to the support bars. Just two are in place now.

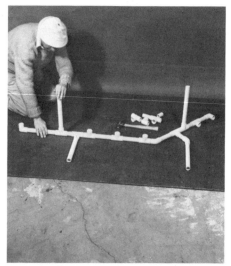

piece; leg T; nipple; support T; 7-inch piece; support T; 7-inch piece; support T; nipple; 45-degree elbow; 7-inch piece; support T; nipple; leg T; 4-inch piece; support T; 5-inch piece; 90-degree elbow. In all, there are two 90-degree elbows, one 45-degree elbow, six support T's, and two leg T's. The support T's hold the support bars that run parallel to the ground when the chaise is assembled. The leg T's hold the legs that run vertically. The elbows can be removed from the ends of the frame.

When one frame has been assembled, and it has been ascertained that all the pipes have been driven all the way into their fittings, the second frame can be assembled. It should be remembered that the two frames or frame sides are mirror images of each other.

Starting at the foot of the chaise, the sequence of frame-side parts runs as shown here.

(Omitting the 90's from the ends of the frame)
11-inch pipe
T
4-inch pipe
T (leg—points down)
Nipple
T
7-inch pipe
T
7-inch pipe
T
Nipple
45-degree elbow
7-inch pipe
T
Nipple
T (leg—points down)
4-inch pipe
T
5-inch pipe
All in all, 19 pieces of pipe and fittings, not
counting the 90-degree elbows that go on the ends

When both frame sides have been assembled, one is placed atop the other with the T's that carry the support bars facing one another. Now a check is made to be sure that each of these T's is in direct line with its mate. If not, one frame is disassembled, and whatever pieces of pipe have to be changed are either shortened or lengthened.

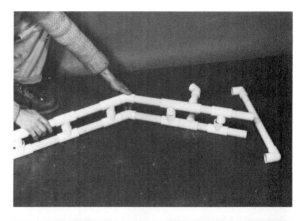

Both frame sides have been assembled. One is placed atop the other to make certain all the fittings line up. Note that the last T on the upper side extends beyond the lower. The upper T is either loose or the preceding piece or pipe is too long.

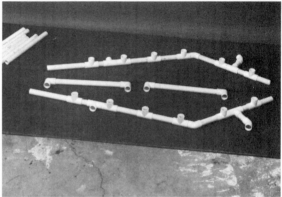

Both frame sides have been assembled completely dry. Here they lie side by side. Note that they are mirror images of each other.

This done, the top halves of the rear legs are slipped into their T fittings. Each of these pieces of pipe are 4 inches long and terminate in 45-degree elbows. Now the two frame sides are laid on the work board. A double check is made, to be sure that all is well before proceeding. The craftsperson may want to couple the frame sides together temporarily, with a few support bars. These are all 17¾ inches long.

Cementing the frame sides   This can begin at either end; it should be borne in mind that the elbows at the ends are fastened to the end support bars and not the frame sides. One frame is turned so that all the support T's point directly upward and the leg T's lie flat on the work board. To make certain of this, a length of pipe is inserted in one leg and another in the support T to be cemented. A straight piece of stick is fastened to the side of the vertical pipe, and then the square is used to make certain that the pipe is truly vertical. The fitting and its pipe are marked. The sides are now disassembled and cemented. Both the primer and the cement can be used on each joint if desired, but the cement alone should suffice. In any case,

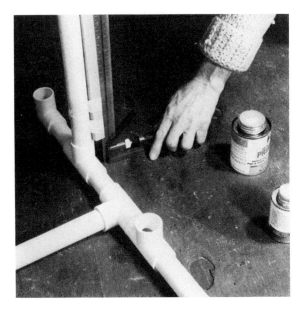

With a piece of pipe temporarily positioned in the T that accepts a leg, the pipes and fittings comprising each frame side are cemented together. The piece of pipe in the upward-facing T is where a support bar will go. The combination square and the piece of wood fastened to the support bar pipe are used to make the support bar perfectly vertical. This bar or scrap piece of pipe is not cemented in. Neither is the elbow visible at the end of the frame side.

the pipe must be driven all the way into the fitting, and the fitting must point in the right direction. This procedure is continued until both frame sides have been assembled and cemented.

At this point assembly and cementing of the two frame sides have been completed. Now, the legs and the braces are to be prepared. The front leg is 11 inches long. The rear leg is assembled from two pieces of pipe and a 45-degree elbow. The upper piece of pipe is 4 inches long, the lower piece 13 inches. The leg brace—the length of pipe that connects the rear leg with the front leg and lies on the ground—is 33½ inches long, but it should be 34 inches long to begin with.

Preparing legs and braces

A 90-degree elbow is fastened to each end of each of these braces; screws are used, and care is taken to keep both elbows parallel to one another. The end of one leg is inserted in one of the elbows. The other end of the brace and its elbow are positioned

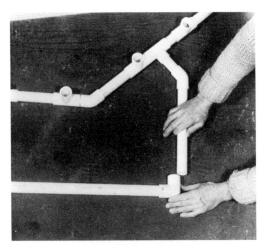

The elbows on the ends of the brace—the bar that rests on the earth—must be screwed or cemented fast to the brace. Here you can see that the brace is a good inch short of the chaise leg. When the leg is forced into the elbow, the pull on the leg by the brace offsets the downward push against the chaise frame by its occupant. Note that none of the legs or their parts have to be fastened to the frame.

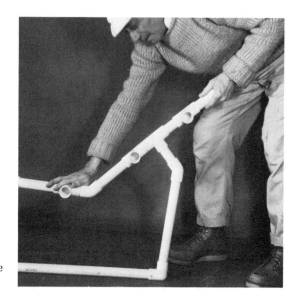

You can test the counter-acting pull of the brace by pushing down on the frame.

near the end of the other leg. The elbow and chaise leg end should not line up. The elbow should be about 1 inch short. If not, one elbow is removed, the pipe is shortened, and the elbow replaced.

Now the leg is forced into the elbow. Doing so will bend the frame side upward, away from the brace. This is what is needed. The same is done for the second frame side and brace. It is not necessary to fasten the legs to the frame or the brace to the legs. But if this is desired, it should not be done now. Wait until you have assembled the entire chaise and have tried it. You may want to shorten the legs to alter the angle of the chaise in relation to the ground.

For a preview of how the frame responds with its legs pulled together by their brace, one frame should be stood up and its middle pushed down on.

Assembling With both frame sides completed the rest of the chaise can be as-
the chaise sembled. Eight support bars are needed, each 17¾ inches long, plus four 90-degree elbows. The elbows are permanently fastened to the ends of two support bars. Screws or cement can be used as

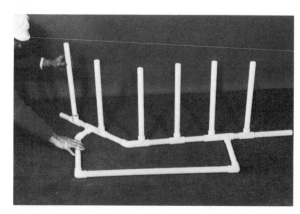

The support bars are slipped into their respective T's. There is no need to fasten them permanently in place.

The elbows on the ends of the end-support bars must be fastened in place. When these bars are slipped into their positions, they hold the entire assembly together. There is no need to fasten the end bars permanently to the rest of the frame, unless you expect kids will pull them off.

desired. The elbows must be parallel. The other six support bars are pushed into their respective T's. Now the remaining two bars with their elbows are placed in position. That is all there is to it. Now the cushion is simply placed on top, and the chaise is ready for the sun or whatever.

All the parts that form the sides of the chaise frame must be fastened together. Screws can be used if desired, but it is best at least to cement the 45-degree elbow to its adjoining nipple and 7-inch pipe; here is where most of the stress must be absorbed. Should one wish to be able to break the balance of the frame sides down, it is inadvisable to break into too many pieces as much time will be spent just figuring out where the pieces go when the chaise is reassembled. If it is necessary to break the sides down, the parts should be limited to three.

DISASSEMBLY

Other than this suggestion, there is nothing more to suggest on disassembly. Only the elbows on the ends of the two support bars and the ends of the braces need to be fastened. All the other parts can be fitted dry.

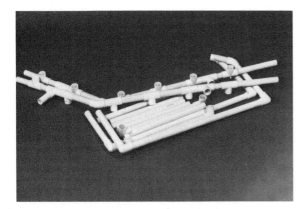

Here is the disassembled chaise sans cushion.

Pipe   1-inch I.D. DWV, 32 feet long, cut into:
         2 32-inch sections
         5 16½-inch sections
         4 15¼-inch sections
         2 12½-inch sections
         6 10½-inch sections
         2 5¾-inch sections
         2 5¼ -inch sections
         10 2-inch sections (nipples)

         ½-inch I.D., 34 feet long, cut into:
         15 18-inch sections
         7 11-inch sections

Fittings (To fit 1-inch I.D. DWV pipe)
         14 T's
         8 90-degree elbows
         4 45-degree elbows

Cushions 2 18½ by 18½ by 2½-inches

The love seat, ready for action.

17. Love Seat

WHEN A PIECE OF furniture for just one provides a comfortless seat without a back it is a stool. When the same bare support can accommodate two bottoms it is called a bench. Put a back to the same Spartan support and it becomes a sexton's bench because everyone knows the hard life a sexton leads. But put cushions on the very same bench and you have a love seat.

Since we have designed the illustrated bench to be used with bottom cushions, it is a love seat: a place for friends, lovers, and friends just warming up to the idea.

As the bench stands, it is 35 inches long, 31 inches high, and 19½ inches deep. The tops of the ½-inch I.D. seat bars on which the cushions rest are 13 inches high. The seat has been planned for two 18½-by-18½-inch cushions, 2½ inches thick, which com-

Corner view of the seat. Note how the same design theme has been carried through almost all the pieces presented in this book.

press to about 2 inches, making the seating surface 15 inches high—the usual height for love seats and their like. The frame is made of 1-inch DWV plastic pipe, except for the seat bars, on which the cushions actually rest, and the back bars where the back will actually rest. These are made of ½-inch pipe, which has an O.D. of ⅝-inch. As will be noted, the cushions are somewhat larger than their supporting surfaces. Thus the cushions overlap the supporting pipes, making for a more comfortable seat and a more attractive appearance—at least we believe so.

The seat can be made to come apart in four sections: back, seat, ends, and center legs. This makes for a relatively flat bundle easily stored or carted off. As with all the other furniture projects described in this book, all the joints can be fastened permanently if desired. Without its cushions, the love seat weighs no more than 25 pounds or so.

VARIATIONS

Size

The love seat is modest in size. Its width and depth can be increased a few inches without destroying its symmetry. The cushions also can be eliminated: it is not too hard a seat without cushions. If this is done, leg height should be increased by 4 or 5 inches to bring seat-bar height up to 17 or 18 inches. On the other hand, if one wishes to add back cushions, the depth of the seat and sides will need to be increased accordingly.

Three-seater

The same design can be followed to build a three- or even four-person seat. The same size of pipe can be used, but an additional set of legs and braces (the bars locking the bottom ends of the legs together) will be needed, plus one change. As the seat sits now, the back extends from end frame (seat end) to end frame, a span of 35 inches. The back will give a bit when the sitters lean against it, but not noticeably. When the back is extended by the width of one person—17 inches or more—the back will flex too much without bracing. One way to brace is to introduce T's into the back bars and the rear seat-frame bar. This sounds complicated but isn't. The three- or four-seater is constructed dry with an unbraced back as long as needed. Now a short length of 1-inch pipe is held vertically against the two horizontal back bars. This is the way each brace goes. Now the back bars can be cut to accept the necesssary T's.

Couch   Couches are usually designed for four or more. They are more "massive" in appearance. We suggest 1¼-inch pipe, so that the frame can be built to accept thicker cushions. For data on various types of day beds, settees, etc., we suggest reference to our *Furniture Buyer's Handbook* (New York: Walker and Co.).

Design   The design presented doesn't lend itself to many variations. The ends or the arms can be made square instead of sloping as they are now. The upper back-frame bar can be lowered and the seven vertical back bars eliminated. In the other direction, the back-frame bar can be raised and the number of vertical bars even increased to fifteen, each one positioned in direct line with the seat bars that run front to back. The arms can be made much lower or even eliminated entirely. In the latter case the end-frame braces would go below the seat frame.

At present the legs terminate in elbows that hold the leg braces. If desired, the legs could terminate in caps and be braced with T's and braces that either run front to back or side to side.

PROCEDURE   As previously suggested, it is advisable to secure the cushions and all the other necessary materials before starting. Then the cushions should be measured, and if they are significantly different in size from those used with this love seat, the seat's dimensions should be altered accordingly. Any cushion less than 1½ inches away from the given dimensions, plus or minus, can be used without problems.

Building the seat   The seat consists of two lengths of 1-inch pipe, called the seat-frame bars for want of a better description. Holes in the bars carry the ½-inch seat bars. Each seat-frame bar consists of a 15¼-inch section of 1-inch pipe. To make the two bars, four pieces of pipe are cemented into two T's. No difficulty here; one need only be careful to insert the pipe ends into the correct T ends.

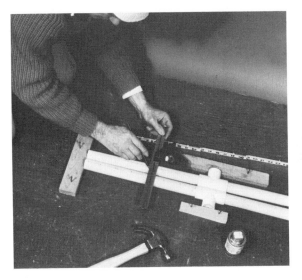

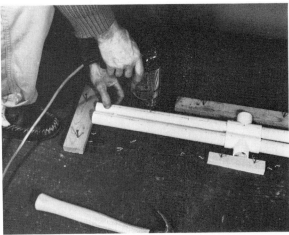

(Above) Pilot holes are drilled through each mark.

The seat-frame bars have been assembled from four 15¼-inch pieces of 1-inch pipe and two T's, cemented together. Now the holes for the seat bars are being laid out. Starting at either end, measure off 2 inches, again and again for the length of the seat frame bars. Note that the central T's point away from each other. Cleats hold the bars aligned.

The two seat-frame bars are placed on the work board, T's pointing away from each other. Cleats are now lightly nailed to the work board to hold the frame bars aligned and in place. Next, a pencil line is drawn down the length of each frame bar. The lines are centered on top of the bars. Starting at any end of the bars, two inches are now measured off, again and again, with a mark on each line. There are now fifteen marks on each seat-frame bar.

Next, a pilot hole is drilled through each mark. Following this, each pilot hole is enlarged to ⅝ inch with a Speedbor bit in the drill. One stands on the pipe while drilling. The drill is held steady with two hands and a very light pressure applied, especially when drilling through the T's.

When all the holes have been drilled, the edges of the holes are sandpapered clean and the pencil marks are erased.

The next step is to cut the ½-inch I.D. pipe into fifteen 18-inch lengths, removing the burrs from the ends of the pipes. The ends of the fifteen pipes—which become the seat bars or slats—are forced into the holes in one seat-frame bar. This picket-fence arrangement is placed on the work board. A couple of cleats are nailed to the board alongside the seat-frame bar. Now the other ends of the seat bars are forced into their respective holes. The easier way to do this is to work one bar into one hole at a time.

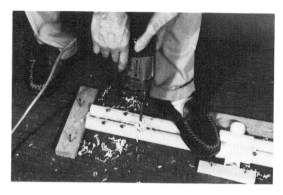

The ⅝-inch Speedbor bit is used to enlarge all the holes. Standing on the pipe helps hold them firmly in place.

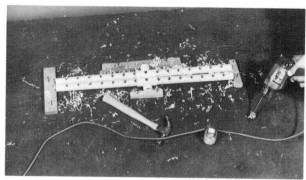

All the holes have been drilled into the two seat-frame bars. Again, note the position of the two T's.

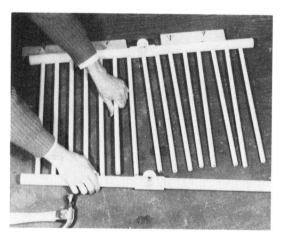

The seat bars are inserted into the frame bars. You need fifteen of these 18-inch long, ½-inch I.D. bars.

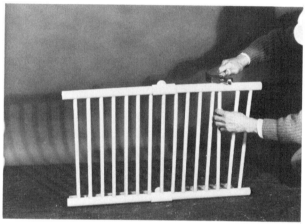

When all the bar ends are in place, stand the seat on edge and drive the seat-frame bars together.

When all the seat bars are in their respective holes, the seat is stood on its side and seat-frame bars lightly hammered toward one another.

Building the end frames   This is begun with two pieces of 1-inch pipe, each 16½ inches long. One T is cemented to one end of each piece of pipe. Now another T is cemented to the other end of each piece. As soon as the T is positioned, the piece of pipe and its two T's are placed flat on the work board. This is done to make both T's perfectly parallel. The dumbbell-looking assembly is now called an end-frame brace—just so that we can easily identify it.

We put the end-frame braces aside for the moment. The seat is placed bottom down on the work board. (At this point, either side

(Left) Assembling and cementing the two end-frame braces. Each piece of 1-inch pipe is 16½ inches long. What is very important here is that the T's on each end of the pipes be parallel to one another.

(Right) T's are slipped onto the ends of the seat-frame bars. They are *not* cemented in place. Nipples are now cemented into the upper ends of the T's.

can be its bottom.) T's are slipped onto the ends of the seat-frame bars. They are neither cemented nor screwed fast into place. Nipples are now cemented into the upper ends of all four T's.

The cement is given a few minutes to harden, and then end-frame braces are cemented in place. This is a double-joint cementing job. A little cement is placed on each nipple, and then the end-frame brace is pressed home. With end-frame braces cemented in place, the seat is stood on its end, and the partially completed end frames are pounded together. This is done just to make certain that all the parts are aligned—meaning that the seat is square and the end T's are tightly in place, still dry.

The seat is turned bottom side up. Pilot holes are drilled through the seat-frame bars, and into the ends of every fourth or fifth seat bar. The hole is enlarged and countersunk. Then a ¾-inch #8 flathead sheet-metal screw is driven into each hole. In this way the seat-frame bars are locked to the seat bars and to each other. This provides front-to-rear bracing and holds the seat together when disassembled.

The end-frame braces are cemented in place. Note that the seat-frame T's point down. Note that you have to cement both joints simultaneously.

The seat frame assembly is stood on end and the end frame—as much as has been put together so far—is hand-pounded down to pull everything together. Note that the end-frame T's (under the craftsperson's fist) has not been cemented in place.

The seat is now turned right side up. The end-frame braces are now higher than the seat itself. Nipples are cemented into the tops of each T forming the ends of the end-frame braces. T's are slipped over the nipples. These T's are *not cemented* to the nipples. They are positioned dry.

The following is very easy to do, although possibly a bit difficult to explain. The lower back-frame bar—a piece of 1-inch pipe, which is 32 inches longer—is slipped into the end of one T sitting atop the end frame. The other end of this long bar is slipped into another T. The second T is now cemented in place. The purpose of this drill is to make certain that the T that has just been cemented is in line with the opposite T. Now the cemented T is allowed to stand for a few minutes. Then the uncemented T is lifted a little, cement applied to the nipple, and the T lowered into place. It should be remembered that the long pipe—the lower back-frame bar—is not cemented to the T's at its ends.

The seat frame is turned right side up. Nipples are cemented into the tops of the T's terminating the seat frame braces. T's with in place nipples are now positioned on top. These T's are *not cemented*.

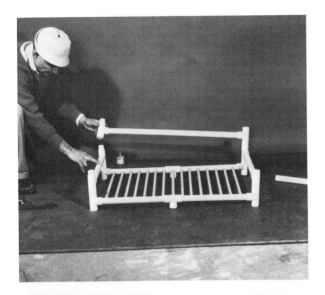

One end of the lower, back-frame bar has been placed dry on its T. A second T (in the craftsperson's hand) is positioned on the end of the 32-inch bar. Now the T is cemented to the T on the end frame. When this joint has hardened, the T on the other end of the back-frame bar is cemented to the end frame. The back bar is *not cemented* to the T's on its ends.

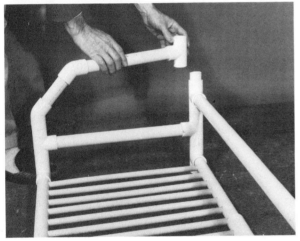

The upper portion of the end frame is assembled dry from two 45-degree elbows, a T, a 5¼ and a 12½-inch piece of pipe.

Next, building the end frame continues. This is done by cementing a nipple into the open end of the T on the front of the end frame. This is followed by a 45-degree elbow positioned *dry*, a 5¼-inch piece of pipe, another 45-degree elbow, and then a 12½-inch piece of pipe. (This may have to be shortened a bit to make it fit.) All these pieces are assembled *dry*. Then, if desired, the long piece of pipe can be cemented to the T, and the short piece of pipe to either 45. The three remaining joints must be cemented simultaneously; it may also be necessary to push the assembly a little to one side to make it straight. This is not easy and really not necessary. All the joints can be left dry if desired. The parts will hold by themselves.

The upper back-frame bar is positioned. The vertical piece of pipe is 5¾ inches long. The pipe is cemented to the T. Then the elbow is cemented to the pipe following the same technique employed to keep the Ts on the lower back-bar lined up.

Completing the back   One back-frame bar is in place. Now it is necessary to position the second and upper back-frame bar. First, two 5¾-inch pieces of pipe are cemented in the open tops of the T's in the corners of the end frames. Then the second back-frame bar is assembled; it is also 32 inches long, and has two terminating elbows. One end of the upper back-frame bar, along with its elbow, is lifted. Cement is applied to the exposed pipe end. The elbow is lowered and the cement allowed to harden. The same is done at the other end; the pipe will flex and permit this. That is all that needs to be done to the back if vertical back-bars are not going to be installed. If they are, instructions are provided a few paragraphs farther along.

The end legs are cemented in place. The center legs are positioned dry. Each leg is 10½ inches long.

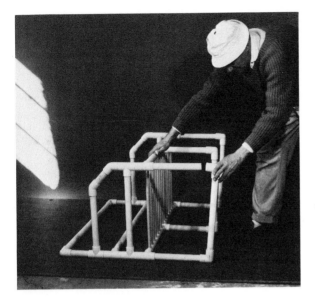

The leg braces, which are all 16½ inches long, are cemented to their elbows and then cemented to the legs. The same technique employed to keep the T's parallel on the ends of the end-frame braces is used to hold the elbows parallel. Both elbows must be cemented to the leg ends at the same time.

Installing the legs

Each leg is 10½ inches long. The four legs that comprise or form a part of the end frames are cemented in place. The two center legs are not.

Next, the leg braces, each 16½ inches long, are cemented to the 90-degree elbows that form their ends. The elbows must be correctly positioned; this is done by following the same procedure suggested for cementing the T-ends of the end-frame braces. Now all the leg braces may be cemented to the seat legs. It should be borne in mind that each brace has two elbows, both of which must be cemented to the leg ends at the same time. So a little cement should be applied to each leg end, and the work done fast.

Locking the end-frames in place

At this moment the end frames are held in place by friction alone—that is to say, the four joints connecting the end-frames to the back and seat are dry. To keep these joints from coming apart, they are locked in place with screws. The alternative is to cement the four joints, which would be very difficult, since four simultaneous joints would have to be made. And, of course, this would also prevent the seat from ever being disassembled.

Installing back bars

At this point, the seat has only two horizontal bars forming its back. To install vertical back-bars or slats, the two back-frame bars are removed. (Let's hope the joints just mentioned haven't been cemented.) They are placed side by side on the work board, aligned, and locked in place with cleats, just as the seat-frame bars were positioned and locked in place. Next, the center of the

If you are not going to install back bars, this is what the seat will look like from the rear, sans cushions. Craftsperson is drilling holes through the end-frame T's and into the back frame bar and then the seat-frame bar. Screws will then be used to hold the seat together.

length of the two bars is found and marked. Then starting at the center, 4 inches are measured off, three times in each direction. This gives the center marks for seven holes, each 4 inches apart, and the middle holes centered on the center of the seat. With the marks as the guide, pilot holes are drilled, then enlarged to ⅝ inch with the Speedbor bit, as before. Seven pieces of ½-inch pipe are cut, each 11 inches long. Next, the pieces of ½-inch pipe are assembled in the holes, just as the seat was assembled.

This done, the back is reinstalled as an assembly. The end frames are locked to the balance of the seat with screws as suggested, and the job is done.

Assembling the back frame. The back-frame bars have drilled to accept the ½-inch I.D. back bars. Each back bar is 11 inches long. There are seven of them, spaced 4 inches apart, with the odd bar in the center of the frame. The same technique used to locate and drill the holes in the seat frame bars was used to drill the holes in the back bars.

The screws holding the end frames to the balance of the seat are   **DISASSEMBLY**
simply removed; the center leg asembly is removed, and the seat
is disassembled.

Index

Numbers in italics indicate illustrations

151